Praise
Developme

MW00778635

"The Leading Student Achievement (LSA) project is one of the longest-standing research projects in Canada. It has been a success because it uses research-informed strategies, is led by a world-recognized researcher, engages the field, and is fully supported by those who are expected to do the work. I commend Ontario principals for having accepted our challenge to adopt a theory-into-practice approach that would expand leadership commitment to inquiry. They have created a legacy that benefits students."

—Avis Glaze, Corwin Author, International Education Adviser, & Founding CEO of the Literacy and Numaracy Secretariat

"Leading improvement at scale is a complex, fraught, and messy business. In this book, Ken Leithwood provides clear, critical insights and sound empirical verification about the ways in which leadership development can be a significant force for lasting change. An intellectual tour de force and a major contribution to the field."

—Alma Harris, Professor of Educational Leadership and Policy, University of Bath, Department of Education

"Having worked with Leading Student Achievement (LSA) and the Ontario Principals Council, and being a longtime fan of Kenneth Leithwood, I have seen firsthand how their work has impacted school leadership across Ontario. Now, in *Leadership Development on a Large Scale* we are able to learn how they did it, which means that their collaborative work will continue to have an impact not only on leadership in Ontario, but on the rest of the world too."

—Peter DeWitt, Professional Development Consultant; Corwin Author; Finding Common Ground blog, Education Week

"There is no doubt that this book identifies a plethora of strategies that will move the field forward. This project has been implemented within a large number of schools/across a large number of leaders. . . . and has been continually evaluated. The strength is that it is not an 'opinion' piece wherein an author references the work of others and then suggests what 'might' be effective, but this is work that has been implemented and is showing promising results."

—Lynn Macan, Visiting Associate Professor & Former Superintendent, University at Albany–SUNY

"After following Fullan, Leithwood, Bryk, and Sharratt for many years, I know this is the next piece in the puzzle of how to implement large-scale school change that has an impact. I love how the project is mindfully constructed to self-assess and is responsive to the feedback from participants. We can learn a lot from reading this book and practicing such mindfulness when it comes to supporting schools to help students learn."

—Linda Vogel, Professor of Educational Leadership & Chair of Leadership: Policy and Development, University of Northern Colorado

"This book examines a major leadership development initiative from which much can be learned. The manuscript is very well organized and written. The evaluation work and findings are technically sound and presented clearly."

—Mark A. Smylie, Corwin Author, Professor Emeritus, University of Illinois at Chicago

"Leithwood demonstrates again why he is the most prominent scholar in the areas of educational leadership and school improvement. He fills a major void in helping us see how leadership can be developed and sustained by providing a marvellous ground-level understanding of how school leadership unfolds and how that knowledge can be used to improve schools."

—Joseph Murphy, Associate Dean; Vanderbilt University; Nashville, TN

"This is a rare book on leadership: grounded, empirical, theoretical, cogent, comprehensive, and unwaveringly true to both local and system needs. As usual, Leithwood 'leads' leadership by capturing the state of play. Dive into *Leadership Development on a Large Scale* and you will be rewarded chapter after chapter with insights and ideas that will improve your efficacy as a leader."

—Michael Fullan, Professor Emeritus, OISE/University of Toronto

"*Leadership Development on a Large Scale* gives us new hope for school reform. Leithwood shows how collaboration between professional associations, a ministry of education, and a team of scholars envisioned, adjusted, documented, and sustained a successful program to improve all the schools in Ontario. There are no quick fixes, as he points to the complexity of shifting a system from top to bottom. There is quiet wisdom in every chapter."

—Karen Seashore, Regents Professor of Organizational Leadership, Policy and Development, University of Minnesota

"Leadership matters. Kenneth Leithwood and the Leading Student Achievement team shine the spotlight on real stories from the field on how school and system leadership is inextricably tied to student achievement and well-being. Our Ontario leadership narrative offers others a pathway to collaborative leading and learning opportunities that lead to improved conditions and success for students."

—Luciana Cardarelli, Program and Member Services Coordinator, Catholic Principals' Council, Ontario

"In 2005, the phrase 'it is lonely at the top' was a general feeling that most school leaders were experiencing in their schools. The Ontario Ministry of Education, under Avis Glaze's leadership of the Literacy and Numeracy Secretariat, welcomed OPC, CPCO, and ADFO's request for funding to structure professional learning for teams of leaders across the province. The impact has been profound. LSA has raised the bar on learning and leading and has had a direct influence on the student learning agenda in Ontario. Ken's involvement at the outset and longitudinal data collection have provided evidence for continued support."

—Joanne Robinson, Thought leader and first Chair of the LSA Project; Director of Professional Learning, Education Leadership Canada; Ontario Principals' Council

"*Leadership Development on a Large Scale* describes LSA as a model of collaboration and research that has evolved in order to guide the work of principals as they seek to improve student achievement. The resources that have come of this project are described by Leithwood in such a way that others wishing to embark on such an all-encompassing project would undoubtedly have a positive impact on school climate, trust, and, subsequently, student achievement."

—Nadine, Trépanier-Bisson, Directrice générale, Association of Directors of Franco-Ontarian Schools (ADFO)

Kenneth Leithwood

LEADERSHIP DEVELOPMENT
on a
LARGE SCALE

Lessons for Long-Term Success

Forewords by Philip Hallinger and John Malloy

A JOINT PUBLICATION

Ontario Principals' Council

FOR INFORMATION:

Corwin

A SAGE Company

2455 Teller Road

Thousand Oaks, California 91320

www.corwin.com

SAGE Ltd.

1 Oliver's Yard

55 City Road

London EC1Y 1SP

United Kingdom

SAGE Pvt. Ltd.

B 1/I 1 Mohan Cooperative Industrial Area

Mathura Road, New Delhi 110 044

India

SAGE Publications Asia-Pacific Pte. Ltd.

3 Church Street

#10–04 Samsung Hub

Singapore 049483

Publisher: Arnis Burvikovs

Development Editor: Desirée A. Bartlett

Editorial Assistant: Eliza B. Erickson

Marketing Manager: Sharon Pendergast

Production Editor: Veronica Stapleton Hooper

Copy Editor: Jared Leighton

Typesetter: C&M Digitals (P) Ltd.

Proofreader: Wendy Jo Dymond

Indexer: Karen Wiley

Cover Designer: Gail Buschman

Printed in the United States of America

Library of Congress Cataloging-in-Publication Data

Names: Leithwood, Kenneth A., author.

Title: Leadership development on a large scale : lessons for long-term success / Kenneth Leithwood.

Description: Thousand Oaks : Sage/Corwin, [2019] | Includes bibliographical references and index.

Forewords by Philip Hallinger and John Malloy
A Joint Publication with the Ontario Principals' Council

Identifiers: LCCN 2018021893 | ISBN 9781544342214 (pbk. : alk. paper)

Subjects: LCSH: Leading Student Achievement (Program) | School management and organization—Ontario. | Educational leadership—Ontario. | Teachers—In-service training—Ontario. | Professional learning communities—Ontario. | Teacher-administrator relationships—Ontario.

Classification: LCC LB2891.O7 L45 2018 | DDC 371.209713—dc23
LC record available at https://lccn.loc.gov/2018021893

This book is printed on acid-free paper.

SUSTAINABLE FORESTRY INITIATIVE

Certified Chain of Custody
Promoting Sustainable Forestry
www.sfiprogram.org
SFI-01268

SFI label applies to text stock

18 19 20 21 22 10 9 8 7 6 5 4 3 2 1

CONTENTS

FOREWORD

The Perspective of a Senior Leadership Scholar

Professor Philip Hallinger, TSDF Chair Professor of Sustainable Leadership, Mahidol University College of Management, Bangkok, Thailand

When Ken Leithwood asked me to give him some feedback on the manuscript for a new book, I was in for a surprise. Intellectual progress in any field follows from the application of creativity, rigor, practical intelligence, and persistence. The scholarship evidenced in this book exemplifies all these qualities. Thus, it comes as no surprise that this volume resonates with and builds on a lineage of research that traces back four or more decades. Indeed, findings that emerge in *Leadership Development on a Large Scale* represent responses to practical problems and research issues first raised in Leithwood's own review of research on the "Principal's Role in Program Improvement," published in 1982. This article was one of the first of its kind to define the direction of a field that came to be known as *school improvement* while also exemplifying the thoughtful and rigorous scholarship that has become Ken's trademark.

This book documents a thirteen-year effort to understand how leadership interacts with other system drivers to produce effects on learning in schools. Although that, by itself, would represent a meaningful contribution, the volume also illuminates how this type of leadership can be developed, enhanced, and multiplied in practice through programs, policies, and practices enacted in school districts. The longitudinal nature of the data or, better yet, *story* that unfolds offers a depth and breadth of insights that seldom accrue from the cross-sectional surveys and short-term qualitative studies that typify research in our field.

A substantial literature has accumulated over the past half-century that affirms that active, skillful leadership is a necessary condition for sustainable school improvement. However, two significant caveats have continued to limit the practical utility of this important finding. First, we have made far less progress on how to develop leaders who exemplify the types of characteristics (e.g., self-efficacy, agency) and skills (e.g., coaching, instructional leadership) described in this literature. Second, we continue to lack examples of how this type of leadership can be enacted on a system-wide basis. This book addresses both of these limiting conditions.

The literature on school leadership development is a persisting embarrassment in the field of educational leadership. Given the large volume of scholarship on this topic, one would expect to find some rich theoretically and empirically grounded insights. Instead, we have a literature that continues to be dominated by prescription, opinion, and endless descriptions of programs. The commonality among these papers is the absence of data provided on program effects in either the short term or the long term. Indeed, until recently, Leithwood's own evaluation of New Orleans's effort to develop school leaders stood as one of the only substantial attempts to study the impact of a leadership development program in education. The good news is that this book goes well beyond that effort by providing theoretically informed, in-depth description and analysis of how leadership can be developed through a cycle of research, development, structured networking, and feedback.

Several substantive observations about the book might also be of interest to readers. First, although research on "leadership effects" is presented, it does not become the dominant focus. Instead, it is woven into the story of how leadership develops over time. Research findings are well complemented by practical applications and "stories" that bring the research to life.

One of the key findings woven throughout the volume concerns the "synergy of small effects." In a world intent on understanding "what works," we often ignore the impact of small supportive factors that allow us to realize the impact of larger, more visible, and significant interventions. As the book aptly describes, this is where values, leader (and teacher) expectations, and human relations lubricate the system so that it can work.

Another notable finding in this volume on leadership is the elaboration of what the theory of action underlying the book calls the "family path." This represents one of the means through which school leaders can influence learning, and the book illustrates how this operates in the real world of schools. I am often asked, "What is the difference between instructional leadership and leadership for learning?" This volume gives me the first meaningful reason to distinguish these related models of school leadership. Simply stated, leading through the Family Path lies outside of the conceptual model of "instructional leadership" but resides comfortably within a conception of "leadership for learning." There is real promise here in finding better ways through which leaders can impact the conditions that influence student learning outside of the school.

Possibly the most useful feature of the book is the focus on a broadly applicable high-impact problem (school improvement, education reform) and the elaboration of how research, practice, lived experience, evaluation, and responses to feedback can cohere into "systemic organizational learning." Please attend closely to the section on knowledge building. The approaches employed in this project offer a useful means for enhancing multilevel learning within the system. Contrary to what many might believe, this book offers evidence that knowledge building, strong as it can be, does not necessarily translate into long-term success. Rather, it requires other supporting factors to be in place to succeed as an approach to long-term school improvement.

This is one of the very valuable features of the book that accrues from "learning about change in practice." The book offers us insights into what works in the short term, medium term, and longer term. This is one of the key features that differentiates this book from other reports. In sum, scholars, policymakers, and practitioners who are interested in issues of school leadership, leader learning, and school improvement will find much to learn in this volume.

Philip Hallinger

FOREWORD

The Perspective of a Senior District Leader

Dr. John Malloy, Director or Education, Toronto District School Board

In the world of education, we need to guard against the propensity to implement ideas, research, and best practices in a "mile wide, inch deep" fashion. No one would argue with our commitment to provide the best learning opportunities for our students and staff, but this commitment demands that we are engaged in a continuous process of learning that is challenging, takes time, and demands perseverance.

I have had the privilege of being part of the Leading Student Achievement project in the province of Ontario since its beginning in 2005. Dr. Ken Leithwood, supported by our Ministry of Education, partnered with our principal associations and district leaders to help us think about how to improve student learning in classrooms, in schools, and across each district. The Leading Student Achievement project has assisted us to think about leadership in different ways. We learned that principals and superintendents play a significant role in mobilizing all educators to share their expertise and leadership so that student learning will improve.

Another important characteristic of the Leading Student Achievement project is the amount of time we have been engaged in this learning, which has informed practice and research. Starting with a small number of boards in the province of Ontario in 2005, it has grown to include most of the boards in Ontario. I think that it is notable that we have been engaged in this project for over thirteen years because many large learning initiatives simply do not persevere this long, and we may find ourselves moving from one new idea to the next. Each year, leaders from schools and districts have been coming together to ask critical questions about how we can support and improve student learning. This group of leaders not only meet together to learn and to collaborate with one another but also make commitments to try different strategies back in their districts. The Leading Student Achievement project does include collaborative inquiry, it does include the gathering of evidence, and the insights that have emerged from this process have informed policy. It is important to note now that the learning has sometimes challenged popular beliefs regarding effective leadership, regarding school improvement, and regarding how students learn best. What I appreciate about the Leading Student Achievement project is that we are not afraid to challenge perceptions and perspectives based on new learning. I am not sure that large-scale learning processes are always willing to challenge widespread attitudes about teaching and learning in the way we did through this project. For example, we all believe that learning teams and networks are very important and that they should be supported in our districts. We learned that though these learning teams are very important, they were not necessarily effective just because people sat in a room together and talked about their practice. With each passing year, as we continued to go deeper with our questions about effective leadership that help students learn better, we continued to develop a better understanding of the conditions that are required for certain strategies to be successful, and most important, we learned that the learning never ends!

So many important insights have emerged from this project and are described in this book. A few notable examples are that having a leadership development strategy is only effective when that strategy is explicitly connected to student learning in classrooms. This leadership development strategy is strengthened by networks both within schools and between schools. We learned about the key learning conditions that are required for student learning to improve and, in turn, where leadership effort should be focused. These key learning conditions include academic press or higher expectations, a disciplinary climate, collective teacher efficacy, trust between teachers and parents and students, and a dogged determination to protect instructional time and to use this time meaningfully and effectively.

By learning together, reflecting on our practice, analyzing the evidence, and sharing our insights with each other, we continued to strengthen and deepen our understanding of effective leadership, which, in turn, supports our students to be the best they can be.

Improvement of schools and student learning is hard work. Large-scale improvement processes are even more complicated because of the commitment to bring about improvement in multiple places and in different contexts. It is so refreshing to be a part of a messy, interesting, challenging process over many years, leading to greater wisdom about how to exercise effective leadership in schools and districts. How different this experience has been compared to the traditional ways we sometimes learn. How important it is to participate with a community of learners over a considerable period who are willing to change attitudes and practices because of what we have learned together. I trust that you will gain many new insights and perspectives in the pages ahead.

John Malloy

PREFACE

School leadership is a significant explanation for differences in student learning across schools. An impressive body of contemporary evidence now points to the dispositions and behaviors of school leaders that contribute to student learning, as well as how those contributions are made. Not surprisingly, this evidence has captured the imagination of contemporary policymakers and educational reformers to an unprecedented extent. School leadership is now widely viewed as both a central explanation for school effectiveness and one of the most powerful levers for improving schools. Belief in the power of good leadership has prompted an enormous number of initiatives, in many parts of the world, to improve the capacities of both aspiring and existing leaders.

The central problem addressed by this book is how to scale up and sustain effective forms of leadership development over long enough periods of time to realize the positive effects on large numbers of students of improved school leadership. This problem includes how to make effective use of good evidence to build, refine, and adapt leadership development initiatives so they contribute to growth in powerful forms of leadership and those conditions in schools that matter most to students.

The central problem addressed by the book is explored in the context of a long-standing leadership development project in Ontario, Canada, called the Leading Student Achievement: Networks for Learning project; its singular goal from the outset has been to improve student success by improving school leadership. Funded by the provincial government's Ministry of Education, the project is led by representatives of the province's three principal associations (French, Catholic, and public): l'Association des directions et directions adjointes des écoles franco-ontariennes, Catholic Principals' Council Ontario, and Ontario Principals' Council. During the thirteen years of the project's history, I have been the project's evaluator and senior advisor. As a team, we have "learned our way forward" with a constantly growing number of the province's sitting principals and vice principals (now numbering about sixteen hundred). To my knowledge, this is the largest and longest-lasting leadership development initiative in the world.

The book unpacks the context for the project (Chapter 1), outlines the evidence used by the project to learn its way forward (Chapter 2), and describes the conception of effective leadership central to the project's development initiatives (Chapter 3). Chapter 4 explores two distinct approaches to leadership development and offers justification for the project's choice. Chapters 5 and 6 argue for the project's commitment to collaborative inquiry as a foundational belief and describe the key learning conditions in schools chosen as a focus for such inquiry.

The project has been guided since its third year by a "theory of action" described in Chapter 7. Chapters 8 and 9 provide an account of the project's work to further its two current priorities: leadership networks and knowledge-building approaches to classroom pedagogy. The final chapter of the book is about lessons from our experience that we believe others aiming to scale up their leadership development efforts would be wise to consider.

This is a scholarly book about a practical project. So the two forewords reflect both perspectives on the book and its contributions. Philip Hallinger provides the scholarly perspective. His long-standing and very influential work on school leadership, leadership development, and educational change has made Phil among the most widely known and respected international researchers in the field. John Malloy provides the practical perspective. John is director (CEO) of the largest school district in Canada and has played a pivotal role in Ontario's efforts to improve the quality of leadership in the province at both district and school levels. The combined insights of Phil and John about the LSA project and the book provide readers with an engaging point of departure.

ACKNOWLEDGMENTS

This book could not have been written without the collaboration of a number of educators and organizations. The Ontario principal associations—L'Association des directions et directions adjointes des écoles franco-ontariennes (ADFO), the Catholic Principals' Council of Ontario (CPCO), and the Ontario Principals' Council (OPC)—gratefully acknowledge the following for their contributions to the writing of this book and support of the Leading Student Achievement (LSA) project:

- Dr. Kenneth Leithwood, Professor Emeritus, Ontario Institute in Studies in Education, University of Toronto, is the author. As project researcher and evaluator throughout the project's history, his knowledge of LSA provides insights into leadership development on a large scale based on evidence gathered over 13 years. LSA deeply appreciates Ken's commitment to research and the recommendations from gathered evidence which provided project leaders and participants with the way forward to building leadership capacity in support of improving student achievement and well-being.

- LSA Coordinators: Mary Cordeiro (CPCO), Ginette Huard (ADFO) and Linda Massey (OPC) and LSA Recorder, Bev Miller (OPC).

- LSA District Facilitators and Consultants

- Ontario Ministry of Education, especially the Literacy and Numeracy Secretariat and the Student Achievement Division, who provided funding and support to the professional learning program of LSA.

- Thousands of educators in districts, especially principals, vice principals and system leaders, as well as directors, teachers and students. From these groups, LSA thanks the authors of the "real" stories of best practices and many participants who shared their learning across the province so all could improve.

PUBLISHER'S ACKNOWLEDGMENTS

Corwin gratefully acknowledges the contributions of the following reviewers:

Clint Heitz
Instructional Coach
Battendorf Community Schools
Battendorf, Iowa

Lynn Macan
Visiting Associate Professor
University at Albany
Albany, New York

Johnny O'Connor
Assistant Professor of Educational Leadership
Lamar University
Beaumont, Texas

Mark A. Smylie
Professor Emeritus of Education
University of Illinois at Chicago
Chicago, Illinois

Linda Vogel
Professor, Educational Leadership & Policy Studies Program
University of Northern Colorado
Greeley, Colorado

ABOUT THE AUTHOR

Dr. Kenneth Leithwood is emeritus professor at OISE/University of Toronto. His research and writing is about school leadership, educational policy, and organizational change. He has published extensively on these topics. For example, he is the senior editor of both the first and second *International Handbooks on Educational Leadership and Administration* (Kluwer Publishers, 1996, 2003). His most recent books include *How School Leaders Contribute to Student Success* (2017, Springer), *Linking Leadership to Student Learning* (2012, Jossey-Bass), *Leading School Turnaround* (2010, Jossey-Bass), *Distributed Leadership: The State of the Evidence* (2009, Routledge), *Leading With Teachers' Emotions in Mind* (2008, Corwin), *Making Schools Smarter* (Corwin, 3rd edition, 2006), and *Teaching for Deep Understanding* (Corwin, 2006). Among his awards, Professor Leithwood is the inaugural recipient of the University of Toronto's Impact on Public Policy award, AERA (Division A) 2011 Outstanding Leadership Researcher Award, the 2012 Roald F. Campbell Lifetime Achievement Award from the University Council for Educational Administration, and the Ontario Principal Councils' Outstanding Contributions to Education Award for 2016. He is a fellow of the Royal Society of Canada. With colleagues, he has completed one of the largest studies of its kind about how state, district, and school-level leadership influences student learning.

Chapter 1

THE LEADING STUDENT ACHIEVEMENT

Networks for Learning Project (LSA)[1]

Talented leadership makes a significant contribution to the success of organizations. Absent such leadership, struggling organizations rarely regain their footing. This claim can now be justified by a considerable body of evidence collected in many different organizational sectors, especially evidence sufficiently fine grained to detect the nuances of organizational change; this claim also has become an article of faith among those responsible for organizational improvement. In education, as in many other sectors, the evidence and widespread belief about leadership contributions have resulted in a veritable tsunami of initiatives aimed at developing leadership capacity.

In spite of the attention driving these initiatives, however, surprisingly little is known about effective leadership development (Hallinger, in press) beyond what we already know about good teaching in almost any adult context. Even more critical, the development of leadership capacity on a large scale—the core problem to be solved if leadership's potential is to be

---

[1]Originally called "Leading Student Achievement: Our Principal Purpose" and later renamed "Leading Student Achievement: Networks for Learning." It is referred to simply as LSA throughout most of the book.

realized—has usually been addressed in ways that have been only loosely connected to the broader reform agendas found in the context of those "being developed." For example, one of the most ambitious large-scale leadership development efforts until recently, England's *National College for School Leadership* (since renamed), was created as an arm's-length agency of the government, not as an integral part of the government's school reform efforts.

This book describes the *Leading Student Achievement* (LSA) project, one approach to the large-scale development of practicing school leaders. Underway in the Canadian province of Ontario for more than a dozen years, the project remains an important component of the province's overall strategy for improving the contribution of public schools to student success. A key goal of this book is to tease out insights from LSA's long and successful experience that might be valuable in other contexts for large-scale leadership development. Such contexts would certainly include other provinces in Canada, leadership development centers wherever they might be found, as well as large districts. The U.S. Every Student Succeeds Act (ESSA), signed into law in 2015, provides opportunities to use federal funds for school leadership development. These opportunities seem likely to encourage large-scale initiatives in states and districts that we believe might also benefit from some of the hard-won insights acquired through LSA's work over the past dozen years.

THE CONTEXT

Ontario's publicly funded school system is an amalgam of four subsystems, including both Catholic and public schools, as well as schools serving both English- and French-speaking students. Seventy-two school districts serve a highly diverse population of approximately 2.1 million K–12 students in vastly different regions ranging from large urban centers (such as Toronto, with 595 schools and students speaking over seventy-five different languages at home) to very small northern communities (e.g., Moose Factory, with one elementary school) serving a majority of aboriginal students. The average district in Ontario includes about thirty-six elementary and ten secondary schools.

During much of the twelve-year period during which LSA has so far been underway, the province's public education system has been widely regarded by some external agencies as among the best in the world (Mourshed, Chijoke, & Barber, 2010). The school system achieved this status during the tenure of a liberal government, elected in 2003 and in power until the summer of 2018, following a decade of conflict and disruption under a conservative government considered by many to be hostile to public education. During both the earlier period of conflict and disruption and continuing through to 2017, districts and schools in the province have been subject to many of the typical trappings of accountability common to jurisdictions in many parts of the world. Those accountability-oriented Ontario initiatives include, for example, mandatory annual provincial testing of all students in Grades 3, 6, 9, and 10, accompanied by provincial growth targets that districts are expected to help meet. During LSA's twelve-year life, begun in 2005, underperforming schools and their leaders have been targeted, as well, for the assistance of provincial "turnaround teams" (Leithwood, Harris, & Strauss, 2010). While not a system of inspection, the Literacy and Numeracy Secretariat of the provincial Ministry of Education, nevertheless, created a large team of "student achievement officers" with a mandate to work in all districts toward improving achievement under the direction of a senior provincial official. These achievement officers worked closely with LSA, as well, as part of their responsibilities. The Literacy and Numeracy Secretariat was the main source of financial support for LSA.

Many policies and procedures introduced during this twelve-year period were primarily aimed at supporting the work of districts and schools rather than simply holding them to account. Especially relevant to the work of the LSA project, these supports included the establishment of a branch of government focused on leadership development, along with the closely aligned Institute for Educational Leadership (IEL). Among the early initiatives of this branch and IEL was the preparation of the Ontario Leadership Framework (OLF), closely based on the best available evidence. The OLF (Leithwood, 2012) provides a set of leadership standards for the province and has been widely adopted by districts, professional administrator associations, and their individual members as a guide to effective practice, a framework for leadership development, and a set of criteria for leadership selection (Pollock, Wang, &

Hauseman, 2017). A summary of the OLF, a central feature of LSA's theory of action, can be found in Chapter 3.

With few exceptions, eligibility for appointment to a principal or vice principal position in Ontario requires five years of successful teaching experience, a graduate degree in a relevant field, and completion of the province's Principal Qualification Program, a two-part program (120 hours each) regulated by the province but delivered by government-approved universities and principal associations. All participants in the LSA program have these qualifications and have been appointed to a formal school leadership position.

These practicing principals and vice principals belong to one of the three professional associations overseeing the project, including the Ontario Principals' Council (OPC) for the 5,237 public school principals and vice principals, the Catholic Principals' Council of Ontario (CPCO) for the 2,165 Catholic school administrators, and the Association des directions et des directions adjointes des ecoles franco-ontariennes (ADFO) for the 565 principals and vice principals in the province's francophone schools. These three professional association have collaborated to guide the LSA project throughout its history with consistent and stable funding from the provincial government. Indeed, the government's unwavering support, along with a climate of cooperation among most of the professional stakeholders in the province over the project's twelve-year duration, to this point, have been critical to the project's impact and spread.

In funding the LSA proposal, the Ministry of Education expressed its belief in the contribution of leadership to school improvement at the school, as well as the district and provincial levels. This chapter begins with a discussion about the extent to which this belief is justified.

THE CONTRIBUTIONS OF LEADERSHIP TO STUDENT LEARNING

Leadership has captured the imagination of contemporary policy makers and educational reformers to an unprecedented extent. It is now widely viewed as both a central explanation for school effectiveness and one of the most powerful levers for improving schools. This belief in the power of good leadership has prompted an enormous number of initiatives, in many parts of the world, to improve the capacities of both aspiring and existing leaders. While the "poster child" for these efforts remains England's *National College for School Leadership*, other very ambitious initiatives are not hard to locate in almost all developed countries (e.g., Huber & West, 2002). Belief in the generative power of good leadership has also stimulated and reinforced advocacy for "distributed" (Leithwood, Mascall, & Strauss, 2009) and "shared" (Pearce & Conger, 2003) conceptions of leadership. If leadership is such a good thing, many reason, the more people doing "it," the better, whether or not they hold formal leadership positions.

As is typical of most efforts to improve schools, the choice of leadership development as a strategy has been only partly rational. While this choice has been undeniably influenced by research evidence, at least as influential has been the contemporary "romance"[2] with leadership, especially in Western societies, a "bias for action" lionized in popular media and the neoliberal-sponsored "new managerialism" turn in public administration (e.g., Peters, 1992). Almost all planned leadership development efforts, however, consume substantial resources and incur significant opportunity costs. In a more fully rational policy world, those advocating leadership development as a strategy for improving student achievement would more carefully weigh the relevant research evidence in helping to sort out the pros and cons of placing their bets on leadership development. Such evidence does not justify leadership development as a stand-alone strategy for improving student achievement. Such evidence does, however, justify including leadership development as a key part of almost any comprehensive large-scale reform strategy. But to realize its potential contribution to an overall reform strategy, leadership development needs to be carefully aligned with other elements of that overall strategy.

A Critical View of the Evidence

Evidence typically cited in support of further developing leadership capacity in schools is predictably less conclusive than such

---

[2]We use this term after Meindl (1995), who argues that leadership provides a simple explanation for organizational behavior that actually has multiple, complex causes.

advocacy would suggest. This evidence has been generated by both quantitative and qualitative studies. The sobering news about evidence from quantitative leadership studies[3] is actually pretty obvious. First, although typically the product of large-scale research, almost all of this evidence reports *relationships* between some set of leadership practices and a selection of valued organizational and student outcomes. Evidence from such correlational research provides only weak support for the sort of causal claims that are foundational to leadership development advocacy. Second, relationships reported in these studies are typically statistically significant but small. Realistically, then, how much improvement in achievement can be expected from marginal expansion of leaders' capacities resulting from well-designed leadership development programs?

Limitations of the evidence produced by qualitative leadership research[4] are equally obvious. While this moderate-sized body of research, unlike its large-scale quantitative sibling, often reports greater gains in student achievement over time attributable to the efforts of talented leaders, the small-scale nature of the studies makes applications to other settings hazardous. Additionally, almost all such studies have used relatively weak "outlier designs." Studies using these designs sample only leadership in schools whose students perform at the extremes of the achievement distribution. These studies do not produce comparable evidence about how much of what is described as "successful" leadership might also be found in less successful schools. As a consequence, these studies tell us something about the "necessary" but not the "sufficient" practices of successful leaders.

Perhaps as serious a weakness, finally, leadership studies using outlier designs begin with the assumption that leadership is a major cause for the improvements in student achievement, as has been demonstrated by the exceptionally performing schools selected for study. Sometimes, evidence confirming the contribution of leadership is collected from teachers or those in other roles, but that is

---

[3]Much of this research has been systematically reviewed in Leithwood and Riehl (2005); Leithwood, Seashore Louis, Wahlstrom, and Anderson (2004); and Marzano, Waters, and McNulty (2006).

[4]A related series of such studies has been reported in Day and Leithwood (2007), for example.

the extent to which this critical starting assumption is tested, and often, it not tested at all. There are many plausible explanations, in addition to leadership, for significant increases in a school's performance. But types of research aside, there is almost no direct evidence linking improvements in leadership, fostered by serious leadership development efforts, to improvements in student achievement.[5]

A More Optimistic Assessment of the Evidence

In spite of this sobering conclusion from the evidence, there remains significant justification for using leadership development as a strategy for improving student achievement. This justification is based on six features of the relevant evidence. First, although typically reporting small effects on or weak relationships with student achievement, the evidence *consistently* indicates that these effects or relationships are both positive and significant. Second, leadership effects reported in the evidence are moderate to large on many organizational variables, which are themselves strongly associated with student learning (e.g., school culture and agreement about school goals). This evidence is in line with claims that leadership effects on students are largely indirect (Hallinger & Heck, 1996; Leithwood & Jantzi, 1999).

In addition, there are no reported instances, of which we are aware, of a failing school turning itself around in the absence of talented leadership. Leadership effects appear to be largest where they are needed most. Furthermore, the database concerning leaderships effects is now at least as impressive in both quantity (roughly one hundred quantitative and many more qualitative studies) and reported effects as are the databases about most other variables selected for attention in school reform efforts—and considerably better than many. Finally, borrowing the concept from Creemers and Reezigt (1996), most school and classroom variables have "synergistic effects." That is, considered independently, their effects may be small, often not larger than the effects reported for school leadership. It is the

---

[5]See Leithwood, Riedlinger, Bauer, and Jantzi (2003) for one of the very few exceptions.

coordinated accumulation of these small effects that can add up to large improvements. School leaders are key stimulators and coordinators of these small effects.

Conclusions From the Evidence

The most reasonable conclusion to be drawn about leadership development as a strategy for improving student achievement is that as a stand-alone strategy, leadership development is unlikely to produce significant gains in student achievement, however well it is implemented. While leadership development might have large effects in some schools, especially (and importantly) in struggling schools, these effects will not be large enough to influence patterns of achievement across a large educational jurisdiction, such as a country, state, province, or even a large district.

Few educational jurisdictions, however, stake their improvement efforts exclusively on leadership development. But this is not the same as embedding leadership development within and aligning it to the more comprehensive reform effort. Since very few jurisdictions have proceeded in this way, the large effects that are possible through synergistic relations across many variables (including leadership), each responsible for small effects, have almost never materialized. Multiple, nonaligned changes in schools have simply produced feelings of confusion, overload, stress, and low morale on the part of school staffs (Leithwood, 2006).

These conclusions and implications based on the evidence suggest a reform strategy that includes but is clearly not limited to leadership development—a strategy in which the parts are carefully aligned. To have their greatest effect, leadership development initiatives should be part of a suite of coordinated strategies, not a stand-alone strategy. Relatively new evidence from research on large-scale reform also points toward two additional features of such a comprehensive strategy. First, it now seems clear that unless leadership development is strongly linked to classroom practice, it will not have much impact. Indeed, much earlier evidence from the restructuring movement in the United States, a movement aimed at increasing the power and capacity of school-level leaders, is a case in point (Beck & Murphy, 1995; Leithwood & Menzies,

1998). Second, a comprehensive strategy that includes leadership development should entail the building of community-like cultures within and across schools (Fullan, 2007).

A BRIEF HISTORY OF THE LEADING STUDENT ACHIEVEMENT PROJECT

In the first year of the project, twenty-two of the seventy-two Ontario district school boards had participants in the LSA project. By the beginning of Year 4, forty-six districts had participants, a total of sixty-nine supervisory officers (second-tier central office leaders), 212 principal learning teams, and nearly 1,700 principals and their schools involved. As of the spring of 2015, the LSA project included participants from sixty-three districts, including a total of 3,210 principals and vice principals and 123 central office leaders.

Launched in 2005, the LSA project was a response to a challenge from the province's Ministry of Education to the provincial school system as a whole:

> *Every student in Ontario will develop reading, writing, math and comprehension skills at a higher level by the age of 12. Progress will be measured by ensuring that 75% of students reach the provincial standard.*

> (Ontario Ministry of Education, 2005)

The three provincial principals' associations initiated the LSA project with a proposal to the Ministry's Literacy and Numeracy Secretariat. The secretariat's subsequent support for the proposal included not just funding but a working relationship with its substantial cadre of student achievement officers, along with access to the services of Curriculum Services Canada (CSC) to provide IT services. The central goal for the project was to further develop those leadership capacities of principals and vice principals needed to help school organizations and their teachers improve student achievement in both literacy and numeracy. In the early years, this focus was limited to achievement in kindergarten to Grade 6 but gradually expanded to all grades.

Since its inception, the project has been based on a multilevel ("trilevel" to begin) approach to providing support to school leaders. At the provincial level, a Steering Team consisting of representatives from ADFO, CPCO, OPC, LNS, and CSC[6] provides overall direction to the project and determines the nature of the support provided to project members, as described more fully in Chapter 4. At the district level, participants were organized into networks called Principal Learning Teams (PLTs), each with eight to ten principals in a team who agreed to meet at least eight times a year. At the beginning of the school year, each PLT was required to submit a learning plan based on the goals of the LSA project and, at year-end, to submit a report on the progress of the PLT over the year. These networks continue to serve as primary and ongoing sources for members' learning and significant avenues for knowledge transfer. At the school level, participating principals and vice principals were encouraged to establish, maintain, and participate in professional learning communities (PLCs); from the beginning of the project, collaborative inquiry in PLCs has been considered key to instructional improvement.

In addition to this trilevel structure, LSA has included a research and evaluation component that has assessed the extent to which LSA priorities are implemented in members' schools and determined if such implementation contributes to student achievement. Results of the annual cycles of research and evaluation are also used to shape future project directions. Chapter 2 describes the nature of this research and evaluation function in more detail.

---

[6]ADFO (Association des directions et directions adjointes des ecole franco-ontariennes) includes principals and vice principals in Ontario's francophone school districts.

OPC (Ontario Principals' Association) includes the principals and vice principals of all English sector public schools.

CPCO (Catholic Principals' Council of Ontario) includes the principals and vice principals of all English sector Catholic schools.

LNS (Leading Student Achievement) is a branch of the provincial Ministry of Education.

CSC (Curriculum Services Council, recently renamed Learnography) provides a variety of supports for learning projects in the province, especially those using sophisticated digital tools.

During the first two years of the project (2005–07), LSA's emphasis was on providing professional learning for participants through relatively standard forms of presentations by leading experts on a variety of ideas that were considered broadly relevant to school improvement at the time (e.g., emotional intelligence). In order to disseminate these ideas at the district level, facilitators' guides and DVDs of these presentations were developed in conjunction with CSC for use by participants.

In the subsequent ten-year period, LSA moved toward the use of much more interactive forms of pedagogy (see Chapter 4), incrementally added many new emphases for participants' attention (summarized in the next section of this chapter), and followed up each of these emphases to determine issues faced in their implementation and their contribution to student learning (see Chapter 2).

By the end of the 2007 school year, the focus of the project became a concentration on "Key Learning Conditions" that robust evidence indicates have powerful and relatively direct effects on student achievement (see Chapter 6). Annual provincial symposia were designed to increase participants' understanding of these Key Learning Conditions and provide planning opportunities for improving them in their own schools. In the 2007–08 school year, many project participants began to work at building their capacities for improving the Key Learning Conditions and to share effective practices for doing this with their colleagues.

The next step in the project's evolution, begun about this time, was further development of LSA's professional networks, web-based technologies, and a focus on collaborative inquiry, specifically the *teaching–learning critical pathway* (TLCP). To support the development of TCLPs, Curriculum Services Canada (now called Learnography) posted a variety of support materials on the project website and assisted LSA in producing a series of web conferences. English and francophone regional sessions, with a specific focus on collaborative inquiry, were introduced to supplement the provincial symposia. Participating principals and district leaders attended two such sessions, accompanied by a teacher leader. Their mandate was to initiate the collaborative inquiry process in their schools.

This process was so successful that, in the 2009–10 school year, the Ministry of Education, in collaboration with LSA, supported a pilot project to introduce collaborative inquiry into secondary schools. Thus began secondary school leaders' participation in the LSA project, participation that has continued with increasing numbers of secondary principals and vice principals since. School leaders involved in the collaborative inquiry process were encouraged to form hubs and networks with those similarly involved. To reflect this growing emphasis, the project was renamed "Leading Student Achievement: Networks for Learning."

The addition of secondary school leaders, along with the introduction by the province of the *Ontario Leadership Framework* (see Chapter 3), prompted efforts to reflect these new circumstances in the project's governance. Representatives of the Ministry's Leadership Branch were added to the Steering Committee, as were members of the branches of the ministries responsible for secondary education (Student Success Branch) and overall student achievement (Student Achievement Division).

Research continued to be a critical component of the LSA project, and in 2010, the evaluator presented the Steering Team with a theory of action to help guide the project based on the project's own accumulation of data (see Chapter 7). This quickly became a key tool used by the Steering Committee to guide future directions and to help project members make better decisions about the focus of their school improvement efforts. The theory of action is considered dynamic and continues to be refined as the project evolves.

By the close of the 2015–16 school year (Year 11), annual activities of the project included the following:

- Two provincial symposia for principals and vice principals

- Provincial symposia for district leaders

- English and francophone regional sessions for all LSA participants in the regions

- District facilitators available to all districts with school leaders involved in the project

- Annual research and evaluation functions

- CSC (Learnography) support through the LSA website, web meetings, virtual sessions, and video production

- Engagement of many project schools in knowledge building approaches to instruction through the leadership of Marlene Scardamalia and Carl Berieter

- A call for proposals to develop, with LSA support, several Networked Improvement Communities (Bryk, Gomez, & Grunow, 2011).

A SUMMARY OF LSA'S PRIORITIES FOR IMPROVEMENT

LSA's priorities for work with school and district leaders include processes believed to foster productive work, as well as specific features of schools and classrooms that warrant leaders' improvement efforts (the "content" or objects of improvement). While attention to processes and objects for improvement has shifted back and forth over time, rarely has a process or object for improvement been discarded. When evidence has indicated disappointing results, efforts have almost always been made to improve, not discard. So in the project's early years, only several processes and objects for improvement were advanced for the attention of members, but by the time of this writing, there were substantial numbers of both.

The project's priorities, accumulated over the life of the project to this writing, are summarized briefly here:

1. *Ministry assistance* with its mission of improving student achievement.

2. *Professional learning communities* (PLCs): A group of teachers and school leaders, often in the same school, who meet together regularly to learn from one another, share their challenges and successes, and work on improving their instruction.

3. *Principal learning teams* (PLTs): A group of school leaders in a district, usually including at least one system leader, as well, with same purposes as professional learning communities but with a focus on improving their own leadership. PLTs often also help guide district as well as school-level decisions.

4. *Collaborative inquiry processes:* Such processes may take several different forms (*teaching–learning critical pathways* and

professional learning cycles are examples), but all include an effort by groups of staff to improve the design of lessons, analyze student work, and create meaningful ways of diagnosing and monitoring student learning. These processes are often the content of the work that takes place in PLCs.

5. *Key learning conditions:* Located in both the school and the classroom, these are conditions experienced by students that are known to have relatively direct effects on their learning and are amenable to improvement through the intentional efforts of school leaders and their teaching colleagues. The LSA project has advocated, in particular, attention to improving the status of conditions labeled academic emphasis; disciplinary climate; focused instruction; relational trust between teachers, parents, and students; teacher collective efficacy; time for instruction (or opportunity to learn); and family educational culture.

6. *Knowledge building:* LSA's most recent initiative, knowledge building, is a theoretically rich and highly developed approach to fostering knowledge creation, global competencies, and student achievement from the earliest years of school. Originating in the work of Marlene Scardamalia and Carl Bereiter, knowledge building is the production and continual improvement of ideas of value to the community. In K–12 contexts, the community is typically the classroom. Idea improvement leads to students' deep understanding of big ideas and complex concepts; students create more powerful ideas and artifacts through use of resource material and bringing their diverse ideas and specializations to the challenge of advancing their community knowledge. The teacher helps students take on high-level activities, such as planning, evaluating, and designing, so that they are positioned to take charge at increasingly high levels. This highly researched initiative has shown significant advances in schools across the Americas, Europe, and the Asia-Pacific region; research consistently demonstrates advances in student achievement, as well as a host of what are currently referred to as twenty-first-century skills and global competencies (Chen & Hong, 2016).

7. *LSA's web-based interactive technologies:* Supported by Learnography, LSA has a website and provides a number of web-based resources for project participants and regularly hosts web conferences.

8. *The Ontario Leadership Framework:* The successful leadership practices that LSA aims to help develop among its participants are described in this framework, a product of the leadership development branch of the Ministry of Education and the Institute for Educational Leadership.

9. *LSA's Theory of Action:* This theory describes the assumptions the LSA project makes about how project initiatives will eventually accomplish the goal of improving student achievement. Described more fully in Chapter 7, this theory assumes that LSA initiatives will improve the quality of school leadership. Such leadership, in turn, will improve the status of key learning conditions in schools, which will contribute positively to student success. Leadership entails assessing the status of conditions on each of those key learning conditions and selecting one or more conditions as a promising focus for improvement at any given time.

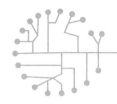

Chapter 2

EVIDENCE USED BY LSA TO LEARN ITS WAY FORWARD

Over the course of its 12 years, to date, decisions on the part of LSA's Steering Team and Board have been heavily informed by substantial amounts of systematically collected evidence. As Chapter 1 indicated, much of this evidence was provided by the project's own research and evaluation results. Annual cycles of research and evaluation have been used to assess the extent to which project priorities have been implemented in members' schools, to estimate the impact of such implementation on schools and students, and to uncover challenges to further implementation that the project might help overcome. Identifying implications of these annual cycles of results for future project directions has been the end goal of this work.

While evidence-informed decision making is a core norm of the LSA project culture, it is much harder to do well than is often acknowledged. Ball (2012) attributes this difficulty to, among other factors, "the inaccessibility of research reports," the "lack of professional norms and time for practitioners and policy makers to consult and use research findings," and "the lack of a forum for equal collaboration between educational practitioners, policy makers, and researchers" (p. 285). LSA's annual evaluation was designed to overcome these difficulties; it was also designed as a response to the skepticism of many practitioners about evidence collected outside their own context and the questionable relevance ("ecological validity") of the results of much research for use as a guide for local practice.

In response to these challenges, LSA's evaluation design closely reflects the central elements of one of four approaches to fostering the use of research in practice identified by Broekkamp and van Hout-Wolters (2007)—the Knowledge Communities Model. This model values collaboration between practitioners and researchers and maintains their traditional roles but "assumes that they work together as a diverse group of actors . . . mutually engaged in a partnership or network of knowledge-exchange as they work to address an educational issue" (Ball, 2012, p. 286).

In addition to LSA's annual evaluations, most LSA leadership development interventions were carefully documented. In the case of symposium presentations, this documentation included video recordings. But most interventions included the development of carefully constructed written records by an LSA staff member (not the primary evaluator) hired specifically for this purpose[1] and often referred to as the resident historian. Ready access to the "in situ" observations and feedback developed by this staff member were an important contribution to the Steering Team's debriefings and the short-term decisions made as a consequence of those debriefings. Steering Team members also have remained close to participants as an important source of informal but quite sensitive feedback about LSA efforts.

LSA's evaluator has worked with the project since partway through the first year. Initially, the evaluator was considered external to the project, providing "summative" evidence to the government funders to assist in decisions about whether or not to continue funding the project from year to year. By the end of the second year of this arrangement, however, the evaluator was repositioned as internal to the project itself, a repositioning considered appropriate by government funders and the LSA leadership team, as well as the evaluator. While this repositioning could be viewed as

---

[1]Beverly Miller.

a significant shift from summative to formative purposes for the evaluation, it did not actually make much difference to the evaluation design. The most significant influence on the evaluation design was the changing focus and priorities of the project.

The remainder of this chapter describes two quite different approaches to LSA's evaluation (Phases 1 and 2) that have been used over the life of the project.

PHASE 1: COMPREHENSIVE ASSESSMENT OF PROJECT IMPLEMENTATION AND OUTCOMES

From 2006 to 2012, LSA's evaluation reflected both of the main perspectives on implementation research described by Century and Cassata (2016), evaluating the *fidelity of implementation* and describing *implementation as conducted*.

Fidelity of Implementation

From a fidelity perspective, evaluation is concerned with assessing the extent of innovation implementation and how well such implementation accomplished its intended outcomes. This component of LSA's evaluation used the same comprehensive pretest and posttest design, collecting quantitative survey and student achievement data as the basis for analysis. Survey data were collected in the fall and spring of each year from participating principals (both elementary and secondary), a sample of their teachers, department heads, and senior district leaders. The two rounds of survey data collection each year required by the first evaluation design seemed manageable for respondents for the first several years of the project but began to be viewed as unnecessarily onerous thereafter.

One sign of this attitude among project participants and their teachers was a gradual erosion in survey response rates. So the evaluation design was modified to accommodate this attitude by collecting survey data only once each year and using the previous year's results as the "pretest," the basis on which changes were estimated. Although this modification introduced some "noise" into evidence about change (some teachers and principals changed schools from one year to the next, for example), the database was large enough to make such noise relatively insignificant.

Each year's fidelity-oriented evaluation component also examined the effects of implementing LSA-sponsored programs and practices on provincial measures of student math and language achievement in Grades 3, 6, 9, and 10. These data were retrieved for all participating leaders' schools.[2] For the first two years of the evaluation, changes in achievement from year to year in LSA participants' schools were compared with changes in achievement with all other schools in the province. This would be the "main effect"—the "quantitative" evidence most obviously justifying ongoing support for the project.

In the absence of finding such a main effect (a very complicated— some would say "impossibly" complicated—thing to do in light of the many other initiatives underway in all districts in the province), the evaluation subsequently has reported the effects on achievement of variation in the implementation of all LSA programs and practices: it has done this repeatedly with very similar results each time. These results have confirmed the value for schools of some LSA programs and practices (e.g., key learning conditions), disconfirmed the value of others, and prompted more nuanced approaches to the implementation of a few (e.g., collaborative inquiry).

During the remainder of this phase of the evaluation, the achievement-related question to be answered became, "To what extent is variation in the implementation of LSA's programs and practices related to variation in student achievement?"

Implementation as Conducted

This component of LSA's annual evaluation aimed at better understanding, explaining, and improving on implementation of LSA's programs and practices. Evidence for these purposes came from

---

[2]Ontario administers tests in these subjects each year through its arm's-length Education Quality and Accountability Office.

approximately hourlong phone interviews conducted in the winter of each year with a sample of twenty to thirty-five school and district leaders. With a focus on LSA's current priorities, these interviews asked about the obstacles schools were experiencing during implementation, strategies school leaders had developed to overcome those obstacles, and the types of support that the project could provide, going forward, to assist with those challenges. By way of illustration, the boxed text "Principal Interview Evidence About TLCP Processes" is a verbatim summary of interview evidence from the 2009–10 annual evaluation report. At that time, a central priority for LSA was fostering "deep learning" among students through the use of an approach to instructional improvement focused on "big ideas" in participants' schools called teaching–learning critical pathways (TLCPs).

Principal Interview Evidence About TLCP Processes

This evidence was provided by twenty-two principals randomly selected from those participating in the project. They were interviewed by phone during the January–February period of 2010.

- Considerable effort was being devoted to implementing TLCP processes with a high degree of fidelity. Many respondents had received training about TLCP processes from Elaine Hine and Denis Maika and were working through each step in the process with their staffs as it had been explained to them. There was some variation, of course. A few principals described modifications in the process designed to make the process more useful (or at least more acceptable) in their unique circumstances. And several principals were relatively new to both the LSA project and the TLCP process. Understandably, these principals were feeling at a loss to answer most questions asked of them by the interviewer. But recency to the project seemed to be the only impediment to significant efforts by school leaders to move the TLCP process forward in their schools.

(Continued)

(Continued)

- Three of the more ambitious aspirations for the TLCP process were being realized, according to the interviews. First, TLCP processes were reported to be having quite positive effects on the further development of the *key learning conditions*. Second, participation with staff in TLCP processes were providing principals with a much better sense of what it means to provide "instructional leadership" in their schools. Third, almost all principals believed that classroom instruction in their schools had improved, sometimes dramatically, as a result of teacher participation in TLCP processes.

- Evidence also identified three TLCP-related challenges. Lack of time for staff to develop the pathways was the most frequently cited challenge. The second challenge was the identification and development of "big ideas." A third and final challenge concerned the level of cognitive complexity required of students grappling with big ideas. This year's interview data shed light only indirectly on this issue, unfortunately. But increasing the cognitive complexity required of students through the instruction they receive is the core purpose for developing TLCPs. Big ideas, by themselves, are only one-half of the central concept giving rise to the TLCP process; deep understanding is the other half.

The Annual Evaluation Reports

For the many years during which the evaluation design was comprehensive of all LSA initiatives (Phase 1), the annual final report assumed a common format. The box that follows contains the table of contents for the 2011–12 report, a table of contents very similar to the contents of reports provided from the first year of the evaluation through to 2012–13.

These reports always began with a summary of results and the recommendations that seemed warranted by those results. This summary was followed by detailed reports of the data from each respondent group and analyses of relationships among key variables that had been measured. Further analyses using student achievement data followed several months later each year to accommodate the availability of Educational Quality and Accountability Office (EQAO) results.

Contents

1. Introduction

2. Recommendations

3. Elementary Principal Survey Results

4. Secondary Principal Survey Results

5. Department Head Survey Results

6. Elementary School Teacher Survey Results

7. Secondary School Teacher Survey Results

8. Relationships

9. Summary of Interviews With School and System Leaders

Appendices

A. Elementary School Principal Survey Analysis

B. Secondary School Principal Survey Analysis

C. Department Head Survey Analysis

D. Elementary School Teacher Survey Analysis

E. Secondary School Teacher Survey Analysis

F. Detailed Report of Interviews With School and System Leaders

G. Teachers' Written Comments

Because the LSA Steering Team was so determined to have their decisions be evidence informed, the recommendations in each annual report played a large part in determining the focus of each subsequent year's project priorities. The excerpted section included in the summary of the 2007–08 evaluation report (boxed section that follows) illustrates the nature of the recommendations to the Steering Team arising from the results of the Phase 1 evaluation design. All annual evaluation reports provided detailed descriptions of the data collected and the analyses carried out but began with summaries of results and recommendations. These summaries were intended to make the full set of data both accessible and manageable to project leaders who relied on them to chart their next steps, a key feature of a knowledge communities model for enhancing research use.

Recommendations Included in the Summary of the 2007–08 Annual Evaluation Report[3]

The results summarized above—and described in more detail in the body of the evaluation report—suggest seven recommendations for consideration by the LSA Steering Group:

1. Maintain the key learning conditions as a priority for project efforts and include development of the key learning conditions among the goals for project-sponsored PD. Such development should focus, in particular, on academic press, focused instruction, and trust in colleagues, parents, and students.

2. Because PLTs seem to be the most powerful source of continuing support and learning for the majority of project participants, significant resources should continue to be devoted to the further development of PLT leaders.

3. Finding time to engage with PLT colleagues and one's staff in PLCs continues to be a challenge for significant numbers of project members. For this reason, the project should consider bringing principals who are still having difficulty finding time for collaborative work in their schools together with colleagues who have worked out useful solutions to this challenge.

4. The LSA project should maintain "effective PLC functioning" as a priority for its continuing attention, with an emphasis on how to

---

[3]This section is copied verbatim from the annual report with only several edits made for clarity. Several sections of the original report have been relocated to make it easier to understand.

sustain already well-functioning PLCs. Evidence continues to indicate that few PLCs have progressed to the point where teachers are observing one another in the classroom, a key practice if PLCs are to have significant consequences for student learning.

5. Since "initiative overload" was a challenge for significant numbers of both principals and teachers, the project should consider helping its members develop "buffering" skills. "Buffering" is an important—but not well understood—successful leadership practice. In the Ontario policy context, buffering is likely to entail greater understanding of the coherence and alignment that exists among initiatives in support of the quite small number of overriding provincial goals.

6. The LSA project should consider adopting, as part of the support it provides its members, a broader focus on "change agentry," with PLCs situated as but one of many components within this broader focus. Developing effective PLCs in one's school will not, by itself, solve all of the challenges a school faces in improving student achievement.

7. *Much could be learned from teachers identified as "resisters" to LSA-related initiatives that would help guide subsequent efforts to further the goals of the LSA project. The Steering Committee might consider whether this would be a good use of project resources*

8. Results of analyses related to student achievement replicate many features of last year's results, adding considerable confidence to our understanding about which school conditions are most worthy of continuing support. According to this now quite robust evidence, special emphasis should continue to be given to the further development of what has now been labeled *academic climate* (academic press and disciplinary climate) in LSA schools. This year's results, unlike last year's, also reflect prior evidence about the importance of two *teacher internal states*, teacher efficacy and trust.

9. As last year's report noted, continuing to position professional learning communities and principal learning teams as the infrastructure for such development is reasonable. But we now have

(Continued)

(Continued)

two sets of very similar results to put in perspective, especially the contribution of PLCs. While clearly one means to the larger ends of the LSA project, PLCs are far from a "high leverage" means, even after sustained, multiyear efforts to implement them well. Perhaps it is time for the project to simply stop making reference to them.

10. School leaders would do well to promote attention to academic climate and teacher internal states among their school colleagues and to use their work with TLCPs as opportunities for that purpose. It is certainly plausible to expect that this year's emphasis on TLCPs will assist the further development of both sets of school conditions.

PHASE 2: TARGETING A SMALL NUMBER OF KEY PRIORITIES

Beginning in 2013–14, the design of the annual evaluations changed from being comprehensive of all LSA current programs and practices to focusing, in a deeper and more targeted way, on just a few especially critical priorities. This reduction in the scope of the evaluation was warranted in part because, by 2013, the evaluation program had accumulated multiple annual data sets about long-standing LSA priorities, which provided considerable justification for their value. The most prominent example of such data concerned what the project refers to as its *key learning conditions* (e.g., academic emphasis, disciplinary climate, teacher trust, collective teacher efficacy, uses of instructional time, and focused instruction). Analyses of the relationship between student achievement and five of the project's "key learning conditions" had produced, more or less, the same magnitude of results for the previous three years (described more fully in Chapter 6).

By the fall of 2014, the purpose of the evaluation had become the development of a much deeper understanding of both the implementation and outcomes of LSA's two highest priorities. That year's evaluation extended previous inquiry about the implementation of knowledge building. As well, a theory of effective leadership networks was developed and subject to empirical testing; this research focus was prompted by considerable evidence from school leaders, over many of the annual evaluations, awarding significant value to principals learning teams. Results about both of these priorities are taken up in more detail in Chapters 8 and 9.

It was during this period that members of the LSA Steering Team became concerned that, while the annual evaluations served most of their central purposes, they did not provide the kind of user-friendly accounts of what LSA schools were actually doing that explained the sense of excitement many school leaders and their staffs were expressing about their LSA-related efforts. This led the Steering Team to issue an invitation to LSA participants to write brief "stories" about their work following a loose set of guidelines provided by the project evaluator, who also served as editor of submissions.

The development of "real stories," some of which appear in subsequent chapters, provided opportunities for LSA members to share their work widely, prompted considerable reflection on the part of story writers, and served to balance the relatively "academic" accounts of LSA efforts embodied in the evaluation reports, with accounts that engaged many people uninfluenced by those academic accounts. At the time of this writing, there have been three annual calls for "real stories" resulting in a total of more than two dozen such stories published in three separate monographs. Taken together, these stories illustrate the form taken in schools by almost all the programs and practices LSA has pursued over the duration of the project. These stories also provide exceptionally engaging samples of evidence about the *implementation as conducted* perspective on project implementation included as part of the first phase of the evaluation.

CONCLUSION

The introduction to this chapter argued that the approach to LSA's project evaluation reflected central features of what Broekkamp and van Hout-Wolters (2007) referred to as a knowledge communities model for fostering the use of research in practice. This approach values collaboration between practitioners and researchers. As the chapter has indicated, the evaluator and the project Steering Team have collaborated to determine the focus of each year's evaluation. While the evaluator has taken the lead on such technical features of the evaluation as instrument design, especially the Steering Team has been consulted extensively on these features. Such consultation has served to ensure that the views of its members are represented and ample opportunities are available to modify technical features of the evaluation to accommodate the circumstances of project members.

LSA's version of a knowledge building communities approach to fostering the use of research in practice has built on the traditional roles of evaluator/researcher and project designer and leader. Recommendations arising from each year's evaluation are just that—recommendations. The Steering Team and Board review results of the annual evaluations themselves, consider the recommendations provided by the evaluator, and make final decisions about next steps for the project. Mutual trust and respect are the key ingredients for making this model of research use productive. The evaluator strives to provide the most robust possible evidence about the project's programs and practices; "holding our feet to the fire" is often how the Steering Team describes the evaluator's role to others. The project's leadership team strives to provide project members with the best possible support for their school improvement work. This interaction among those in traditional roles reflects the nature of relationships that are fundamental to a knowledge building model that, as Ball argues, "assumes that [policy makers and researchers] work together as a diverse group of actors . . . mutually engaged in a partnership or network of knowledge-exchange as they work to address an educational issue" (2012, p. 286).

Chapter 3

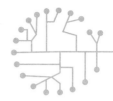

BUILDING ON A SHARED UNDERSTANDING OF EFFECTIVE SCHOOL LEADERSHIP

From the beginning of the project, LSA's single and unchanging goal has been to increase student achievement (the distal or long-term goal) by improving the quality of leadership in its members' schools (the proximal or short-term goal). Of course, accomplishing this goal depends on having an explicit, widely endorsed account of effective leadership justified by a robust body of evidence. For such an account, LSA has consistently relied on work undertaken by the province's Ministry of Education rather than attempting to develop such an account by itself.

Beginning with a commitment to improving school leadership included in the initial platform of a liberal government newly elected in 2003, several rounds of development work were undertaken over a nine-year period to provide the province with an evidence-based description of effective school and district leadership.

These efforts paralleled considerable work in other provinces and countries to develop leadership "standards" for guiding the selection, development, and evaluation of leaders.[1] The work undertaken in Ontario culminated in 2012 with the still-current publication of the Ontario Leadership Framework (OLF; Leithwood, 2012). This account of effective leadership has recently been judged among the most comprehensive, evidence-based accounts of effective school leaders' practices available (Hitt & Tucker, 2016).

The OLF defines leadership as "the exercise of influence on organizational members and diverse stakeholders toward the identification and achievement of the organization's vision and goals" (p. 3). Leadership is exercised through relationships between and among individuals who may or may not hold formal leadership positions, although the focus of LSA's work has always been on principals and vice principals. This chapter of the book provides a brief summary of the school leader section of the OLF (there is also a section about district-level leadership) describing effective leadership practices, as well as "personal leadership resources."[2]

SUCCESSFUL LEADERSHIP PRACTICES[3]

The approach to school-level leadership outlined in the OLF does not align itself with any specific leadership model or theory. While leadership models and theories provide a conceptual coherence which can assist in building understanding, no existing individual theory or model captures a sufficient proportion of what leaders actually do to serve the purposes intended for the OLF. That said, the OLF does reflect most of the practices found in current models of both "instructional" and "transformational" leadership. Using a term that has become common in the educational leadership literature, it is an "integrated" model (for example, see Printy, Marks, &

---

[1]By now there are many sets of such standards, for example, the U.S. Professional Standards for School Leaders (National Policy Board for Educational Administration [NPBEA], 2015), the UK National Standards for School Leadership (National College for School Leadership [NCSL], 2008) and the Australian Standard for School Principals (Australian Institute for Teaching and School Leadership [AITSL], 2015).

[2]For citations of evidence justifying what is described in the following, see the original OLF.

[3]Parts of this section are based on Leithwood, Sun, and Pollock (2017).

Bowers, 2010), although a more fully developed one than appears in most literature to date. This integrated model aims to capture the relatively direct efforts of successful leaders to improve the quality of teaching and learning in their schools (the primary focus of instructional leadership models), as well as their efforts to create organizational conditions that enable and support those improvement efforts (the primary focus of transformational leadership models).

Table 3.1 describes the five domains of practices outlined in the OLF. Each of these domains includes a handful of more specific practices, twenty-one in total. These more specific practices are closely aligned to evidence about successful leadership, whereas the domains are best thought of as conceptual organizers that aid framework users' sense-making and memory.

In addition, each of the twenty-one specific practices is further illustrated, as in Table 3.2, using just two of the leadership practices. This level of specification is described for all twenty-one leadership practices in the OLF itself.

One of the more complex challenges facing those developing leadership frameworks and standards is to determine the appropriate level of specification. Where is the "sweet spot" between a level of specification that generalizes to almost all leaders and their circumstances (e.g., all elementary and secondary school principals in a state or province) and one that is relevant for only one set of leaders and their circumstances (e.g., secondary school department heads working with urban students from economically disadvantaged families).

Framework developers are rarely explicit about how they address this challenge, and there is no formula to help. The recently revised U.S. standards (NPBEA, 2015) include two levels of specification, for example, whereas the OLF includes three levels: domains of practice, successful leadership practices associated with each domain, and illustrations of how to use each of the successful leadership practices. Settling on three levels for the OLF was simply a matter of responding to many rounds of feedback provided during the framework development process from practicing leaders and those who worked with them about the need for greater clarity about what each practice entailed "on the ground."

TABLE 3.1 What Successful School Leaders Do

DOMAINS OF PRACTICE	SPECIFIC PRACTICES
Set Directions	• Build a shared vision
	• Identify specific, shared, short-term goals
	• Create high-performance expectations
	• Communicate the vision and goals
Build Relationships and Develop People	• Stimulate growth in the professional capacities of staff
	• Provide support and demonstrate consideration for individual staff members
	• Model the school's values and practices
	• Build trusting relationships with and among staff, students, and parents
	• Establish productive working relationships with teacher federation representatives
Develop the Organization to Support Desired Practices	• Build collaborative cultures and distribute leadership
	• Structure the organization to facilitate collaboration
	• Build productive relationships with families and communities
	• Connect the school to its wider environment
	• Maintain a safe and healthy school environment
	• Allocate resources in support of the school's vision and goals
Improve the Instructional Program	• Staff the instructional program
	• Provide instructional support
	• Monitor student learning and school improvement progress
	• Buffer staff from distractions to their work
Secure Accountability	• Build staff members' sense of internal accountability
	• Meet the demands for external accountability

Domains of Practice

The first level of specification describes domains or categories that encompass underlying theories or explanation for why the described leadership practices are successful. In addition to offering a conceptual explanation for successful leadership practices, identification of domains makes a framework memorable and adds considerable meaning to the framework for those who are its intended users. For most of these purposes, whether or not the domains can be empirically justified, as in the case of the factor analysis underlying McREL's framework (Waters & Cameron, 2007), is not critical. Left at the level of twenty-one "responsibilities," the McREL framework is decidedly not memorable and very difficult to make sense of.

Each of the leadership practices described in the OLF reflects one of five broad domains or categories: Setting Directions, Building Relationships and Developing People, Developing the Organization to Support Desired Practices, Improving the Instructional Program, and Securing Accountability. The first three of these domains originate in two sources. One source is a corpus of empirical research accumulated over at least three decades identifying a set of practices that are core or essential across many organizational contexts and sectors (Leithwood, 1994; Leithwood & Riehl, 2005; Yukl, 1994). The second source is what Rowan, Fang-Chen, and Miller (1997) described as "decades of research on teaching" that explains variation in teachers' contributions to student achievement (teachers' performance, or P) as a function of their knowledge and skill (ability, or A), their motivation (M), and the settings in which they work (S): this explanation is captured succinctly in the formula $P = f(A, M, S)$.

Both sources cited earlier point to key functions of leaders as assisting their teachers and other organizational colleagues to further develop their motivations (one of the primary purposes for Setting Directions) and abilities (the purpose for Building Relationships and Developing People) to accomplish organizational goals, as well as to create and sustain supportive work settings (the goal of Developing the Organization to Sustain Desired Practices). In addition, every organization has a unique "technology" for accomplishing its primary purposes, and the fourth domain of practices included in the OLF, Improving the Instructional Program, reflects that "technology" for schools (teaching and learning). Finally, the fifth domain of OLF, Securing Accountability, is justified by the policy context in which contemporary public schooling finds itself, one which places unprecedented demands on leaders to publicly demonstrate the progress being made toward accomplishing the purposes established for their organizations.

Specific Leadership Practices

The second level of specification, appearing in the right column of Table 3.1, describes successful leadership practices within each of the five domains close to the detail used in the research identifying each of the practices. At this level, fidelity to the relevant empirical research is paramount. OLF's claim to be evidence-based is largely justified by the explicit nature of the links it makes between high-quality empirical evidence and each of the twenty-one successful leadership practices. For an explicit discussion of these links, see the original OLF document (Leithwood, 2012).

The third level of specification, illustrated in Table 3.2 (and fully described in the OLF itself), outlines how each of the successful leadership practices could be enacted in some relevant context. Evidence for these illustrative enactments can be found in much of the qualitative educational leadership literature. The shift from "what" leaders do to "how" they do it, however, is much less distinct than such language seems to suggest. Every attempt to describe how a leadership practice might be carried out could be followed by a request for ever more detail prompted by variation in leaders' contexts. One person's "how" is another person's "what."

The value of OLF practices depends, finally, on leaders enacting the practices in ways that are sensitive to the specific features of the settings in which they work, the people with whom they are working, and changes over time (Hallinger, 2016). So the OLF stops at three levels of specification, arguing that those using the OLF are expected to bring considerable local knowledge and problem-solving expertise to the enactment of the successful leadership practices. This expectation acknowledges the necessarily contingent nature of leaders' work in the dynamic environments of schools.

TABLE 3.2 From What to How: Two Examples

DOMAIN: SETTING DIRECTIONS
WHAT: *BUILDING A SHARED VISION*

HOW

- Establish, with staff, students, and other stakeholders, an overall sense of purpose or vision for work in their schools to which they are all strongly committed.
- Build understanding of the specific implications of the schools' vision for its programs and the nature of classroom instruction.
- Encourage the development of organizational norms that support openness to change in the direction of that purpose or vision.
- Help staff and other stakeholders to understand the relationship between their schools' vision and board and provincial policy initiatives and priorities.

DOMAIN: BUILD RELATIONSHIPS AND DEVELOP PEOPLE
WHAT: *STIMULATE GROWTH IN THE PROFESSIONAL CAPACITIES OF STAFF*

HOW

- Encourage staff to reflect on what they are trying to achieve with students and how they are doing it.
- Lead discussions about the relative merits of current and alternative practices.
- Challenge staff to reexamine the extent to which their practices contribute to the learning and well-being of all of their students.
- Facilitate opportunities for staff to learn from each other.
- Be a source of new ideas for staff learning.
- Encourage staff to pursue their own goals for professional learning.
- Encourage staff to develop and review their own professional growth goals and their relationship to school goals and priorities.
- Encourage staff to try new practices consistent with their own interests.

PERSONAL LEADERSHIP RESOURCES

In addition to those successful leadership practices summarized in Tables 3.1 and 3.2, the OLF includes a small but critical number of personal resources or qualities that leaders draw on as they enact effective leadership practices and that, in turn, are shaped by those enactment experiences. Considered together, these resources substantially overlap with some of the leadership "traits" that preoccupied early leadership research and that lately have proven to be powerful explanations for leaders' success. Leadership traits have been defined broadly as "relatively stable and coherent integrations of personal characteristics that foster a consistent pattern of leadership performance across a variety of group and organizational situations" (Zaccaro, Kemp, & Bader, 2004).

While many traits or personal characteristics have been associated with leaders and leadership, the OLF includes only those for which there is compelling empirical evidence suggesting that they are instrumental to leadership success. Titled *personal leadership resources* in the OLF (and often referred to by Ontario leaders now as PLRs), they are of three types—cognitive, social, and psychological, as summarized in Table 3.3.

Cognitive Resources

Considerable evidence collected over many decades suggests that leaders' effectiveness is partly explained by intelligence and experience. This would only be surprising if it was not the case, although some early evidence indicates that stressful and hectic environments (features of environments in which school leaders often find themselves) reduce the advantage of greater intelligence to near zero. Intelligence and experience, however, are "surface" traits of

TABLE 3.3 OLF's Personal Leadership Resources

Cognitive Resources	• Problem-solving expertise
	• Domain-specific knowledge
	• Systems thinking
Social Resources	• Perceiving emotions
	• Managing emotions
	• Acting in emotionally appropriate ways
Psychological Resources	• Optimism
	• Self-efficacy
	• Resilience
	• Proactivity

leaders offering little guidance to those selecting and developing leaders or to leaders and aspiring leaders themselves. Below the surface of what is typically referred to as leader's intelligence are problem-solving capacities and below the surface of "experience" is the "domain-specific" knowledge useful for such problem solving; the OLF includes both as "cognitive resources."

Problem-Solving Expertise

The literature on expert problem-solving processes includes some variation in component processes or skills. For example, one approach, based on research with school leaders (Leithwood & Steinbach, 1995) includes such processes as problem interpretation, goal setting, weighing principles and values, clarifying constraints, developing solution processes, and controlling one's mood (expertise within these processes is described in the OLF). Another approach, based on research largely in nonschool sectors (Mumford, Bedell, Hunter, Espejo, & Boatman, 2006), includes similar though fewer processes, including identifying the causes of the problem, determining the resources available to solve the problem, diagnosing the restrictions on one's choice of actions, and clarifying contingencies.

Evidence about problem solving highlighted in the OLF is primarily concerned with how leaders solve "unstructured" problems, the nonroutine problems requiring significantly more than the application of existing know-how, or what is sometimes referred to as *adaptive leadership*. Results of this research offer powerful guidelines for how to deal productively with the truly thorny challenges faced by those exercising leadership. Much of LSA's effort to build collaborative inquiry skills among its members illustrate the variety of useful approaches that can be taken to build leaders problem-solving capacities.

Domain-Specific Knowledge

Because school leaders' influence on student learning is largely indirect, knowledge about school and classroom conditions with significant effects on students that can be influenced by school leaders is an extremely important aspect of what leaders need to know. Indeed, "leadership for learning" can be described relatively simply—but accurately—as the process of (a) diagnosing the status of potentially powerful learning conditions in the school and classroom, (b) selecting those learning conditions most likely to be constraining student learning in one's school, and (c) improving the status of those learning conditions. One of LSA's main priorities (key learning conditions) over its twelve-year history has been the development of such knowledge among its members.

Systems Thinking

Systems thinking includes the ability and willingness to better understand the connections among different policies, practices, and structures in one's organization and to consider the long-term effects and side effects of one's decisions.

Social Resources

The importance attached to leaders' social resources has a long history. Early efforts to theorize leadership carried out at Ohio and Michigan State universities in the 1950s and 1960s situated relationship building among the two or three most important dimensions of effective leadership. More recently, Goleman has claimed that empathy "represents the foundation skill for all social competencies important for work" (Sadri, Weber, & Gentry, 2011, p. 819). Transformational leadership theory includes a focus on "individualized consideration," and leader–member exchange theory (Erdogen & Liden, 2002) argues that leadership effectiveness depends on building differentiated relationships with each of one's colleagues, relationships that reflect their individual needs, desires, and capacities.

Social resources encompass the leader's ability to understand the feelings, thoughts, and behaviors of persons, including oneself, in interpersonal situations and to act appropriately on that understanding. The three sets of social resources included in the OLF (summarized in Table 3.3) are perceiving emotions, managing emotions, and acting productively in response to their own and others' emotions. Enacting these social resources helps build a positive emotional climate in the school, an important mediator of leaders' impacts on the performance of their organizations.

Perceiving Emotions

Perceiving emotions includes the ability to detect, from a wide array of clues, one's own emotions (self-awareness) and the emotions of others. People with this social resource are able to recognize their own emotional responses and how those emotional responses shape their focus of attention and influence their actions. They are also able to discern the emotions being experienced by others, for example, from their tone of voice, facial expressions, body language, and other verbal and nonverbal information.

Managing Emotions

Managing emotions includes managing one's own and others' emotions, including the interaction of emotions on the part of different people in pairs and groups. People with this relational resource are able to understand the reasons for their own "intuitive" emotional responses and are able to reflect on the potential consequences of those responses; they are also able to persuade others to be more reflective about their own "intuitive" emotional responses and to reflect on the potential consequences of those responses.

Acting in Emotionally Appropriate Ways

Acting in emotionally appropriate ways entails the ability to respond to the emotions of others in ways that support the purposes for the interaction. This social resource allows leaders to exercise a high level of cognitive control over which emotions are allowed to guide their actions and to assist others to act on emotions most likely to best serve their interests.

Psychological Resources

The three psychological resources included in the OLF are optimism, self-efficacy, and resilience. While evidence suggests that each of these resources make significant contributions to leadership initiatives responsible for risk-taking and eventual success (e.g., Avey, Wernsing, & Luthans, 2008), a recent line of theory and research argues that when the three resources act in synergy— that is, when one person possesses all three resources—they make an especially large contribution to leadership success.

Optimism

Optimism is the habitual expectation of success in one's efforts to address challenges and confront change now and in the future.

Optimistic leaders habitually expect good things to result from their initiatives while pessimistic leaders habitually assume that their efforts will be thwarted, as often as not. When the expectations of optimistic leaders are not met, they pursue alternative paths to accomplish their goals. Optimistic leaders expect their efforts to be successful in relation to those things over which they have direct influence or control but not necessarily to be powerful enough to overcome negative forces in their organizations over which they have little or no influence or control; they are realistic as well as optimistic. Optimistic leaders are likely to take initiative and responsible risks with positive expectations regardless of past problems or setbacks.

Self-Efficacy

Self-efficacy is a belief about one's own ability to perform a task or achieve a goal. It is a belief about ability, not actual ability. That is, efficacious leaders believe they have the ability to solve whatever challenges, hurdles, or problems that might come their way in their efforts to help their organizations succeed. Self-efficacy beliefs contribute to leaders' success through their directive effects on leaders' choices of activities and settings and can affect coping efforts once those activities are begun. Efficacy beliefs determine how much risk people will take, how much effort they will expend, and how long they will persist in the face of failure or difficulty. The stronger the self-efficacy, the longer the persistence. Leadership self-efficacy or confidence, it has been claimed, is likely the key cognitive variable regulating leader functioning in a dynamic environment and has a very strong relationship with a leader's performance. Leaders' collective efficacy, developed in the LSA project through leadership networks, for example, is also a powerful, shared leadership resource.

Resilience

Resilience is the ability to recover from or adjust easily to misfortune or change. Resilience is significantly assisted by high levels of efficacy but goes beyond the belief in one's capacity to achieve in the long run. At the core of resilience is the ability to "bounce back" from failure and even move beyond one's initial goals while doing so. Resilient leaders or potential leaders have the ability to thrive in the challenging circumstances commonly encountered by school leaders.

CONCLUSION

LSA's adoption of the Ontario Leadership Framework as its own explicit account of the forms of leadership it aimed to develop had a number of important advantages for both the project and the province. Most obviously, it eliminated the need for LSA to spend resources on developing its own account of effective leadership. It also ensured coherence between its leadership efforts and the many other district and provincial leadership development programs underway in the province. As a program run by the province's three principal associations, LSA's adoption of the OLF also guaranteed a level of OLF use by school and district leaders across the province that the Ministry of Education by itself would have had great difficulty accomplishing.

Adoption and use by LSA of the Ontario Leadership Framework serves as a powerful example of how the project functioned as, what Chapter 4 describes in more detail, an "accelerator" and "catalyst" of professional development for school leaders.

Chapter 4

LSA'S APPROACH TO LEADERSHIP DEVELOPMENT

LSA's initial approach to its work was informed by a vision and framework that mirrored many features of the provincial government's own view of large-scale improvement. This chapter begins with an outline of that framework and is followed by a description of two different perspectives on LSA's work. These two different perspectives help explain the project's evolution. The chapter concludes with a summary of the central components of LSA's leadership development program.

LSA'S INITIAL VISION AND FRAMEWORK

The conclusion from Chapter 1 that leadership development can be a useful part of a larger improvement agenda that includes careful alignment of efforts was at least clearly understood by those launching and funding the LSA project. This understanding helps explain not only many of LSA's choices of priorities but also the inclusion on LSA's board of representatives of agencies also sharing responsibility for the province's larger improvement agenda.

The LSA project envisioned principals collaborating, in both district-level principal learning teams and school-level professional learning communities, for the purpose of improving instructional practice and student achievement. This vision was based on the assumption that "there is no chance that large-scale improvement will happen, let alone stick, unless capacity building is a central component of any strategy for improvement." The vision assumed, as well, that "capacity building *throughout the system* at all levels must be developed in concert, and doing this requires powerful new system forces" (Fullan, 2006, p. 10, italics in original).

The LSA project created an infrastructure that integrated "top-down and bottom-up forces in an ongoing, dynamic manner" (Fullan, 2006, p. 95) that encouraged leaders at all three levels— school, district, and province—to interact together to build their collective capacities. The three overlapping circles in Figure 4.1, included in LSA's early project descriptions, suggest a commitment

FIGURE 4.1 LSA Triad: Trilevel Collaborative Leadership

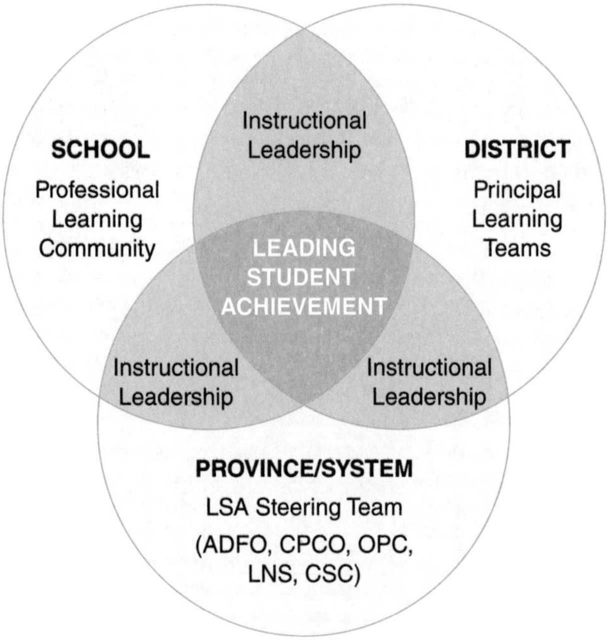

Note: ADFO = l'Association des directins et directions adjointes des écoles franco-ontariennes; CPCO = Catholic Principals' Council Ontario; OPC = Ontario Principals' Council; LNS = Leading Student Achievement; CSC = Curriculum Services Canada.

to the dynamic interaction necessary for supporting collective leadership learning on a system-wide scale.

As the figure suggests, cross-level collaborative leadership was considered central to the operation of the project. At the provincial level, the Steering Team was to provide system-wide leadership by developing and facilitating a variety of professional learning opportunities for principals and vice principals. At the district level, principals were to work in principal learning teams, usually with at least one district leader, to increase their capacities as instructional leaders and as leaders of professional learning communities. At the school level, principals were to support teacher learning teams in their efforts to improve instructional practice and to raise student achievement.

As described in Chapter 7, this initial framework evolved and changed in response to changes in the larger provincial improvement strategy and especially in response to research about how leadership development could make a greater contribution to the overall improvement effort. This was research found in the broader literature, as well as—and especially—evidence emerging from the project's own annual evaluations.

COMPLEMENTARY PERSPECTIVES ON LSA'S FUNCTIONS

As the stimulus for creating the project and the framework guiding its early work indicates, the project is a hybrid of two more common approaches to school improvement. It has many features of a large-scale program for the professional development of school leaders, as well as attributes typically associated with widespread implementation of innovative educational policies and practices. Viewing LSA from both perspectives provides a fuller understanding of the nature of its work, the effects it has had in participants' schools, and the project's endurance.

LSA as a Provider, an Accelerator, and a Catalyst of Professional Development for School Leaders

Leadership development on a large scale, one perspective on LSA's function, introduces unique challenges that small-scale leadership development efforts do not face. The most obvious of these challenges is how to reach large numbers of school leaders with professional development experiences that are both meaningful and sufficiently focused and intense that changes in participants' practices are likely. This is an enormous challenge when viewed from the relatively narrow perspective currently dominating the literature about successful leadership development (e.g., Miller et al., 2016; Winn et al., 2016). This perspective, clearly a valuable one in some contexts, aims to identify features of effective formal programs typically offered as part of a university graduate degree, by an alternative program provider (e.g., The National Institute for School Leadership Executive Development Program; New Leaders' Aspiring Principals Preparation Program: Leadership Policy Institute), or by a stand-alone institution for leadership development (e.g., Greater New Orleans School Leadership Center).

Professional development (PD), however, occurs across a continuum, from formal to informal (Kindt, Gijbels, Grosemans, & Donch, 2016), and the focus of much of the current literature about school leader development is about the formal end of the continuum, a preoccupation with decisions about predetermined goals, fixed time frames, explicit curricula, and planned pedagogy. LSA's approach to leadership development included features associated with the narrow or largely formal perspective described previously; LSA "provided" formal PD experiences for participating school leaders, and the nature of that PD is described later in this chapter. But LSA also influenced less formal or informal types of leaders' professional development.

As Rogoff, Callanan, Gutierrez, and Erickson (2016) explain, informal learning "is non-didactic, is embedded in meaningful activity, builds on the learner's initiative, interest, or choice . . . and does not involve assessment external to the activity" (p. 358). Informal learning is shaped by "authentic activity" and is interactive. A significant portion of the guidance for this form of learning typically comes from others learning in the same context, and together, they "hone their existing knowledge and skills and also innovate, developing new ideas and skills" (Murphy & Knight, 2016, p. 360).

LSA's approach to leadership development stimulated informal learning in two ways. One of these ways was to act as an "accelerator" for other forms of PD experienced by school leaders, not least leaders' own personally defined professional learning. LSA's theory of action (Chapter 7), for example, was adopted by many LSA participants as a framework to guide their school improvement efforts. This framework shaped the goals of those improvement efforts, encouraged a focus on the improvement of conditions in schools that considerable formal evidence indicated matter most to student success, and helped determine for many school leaders what should be the content of their own professional learning plans. Other examples of LSA's "accelerator" effect on leaders' learning are evident in the design of those elements of LSA's formal program designed as models that leaders might use in their schools to engage teachers in productive professional development. Some of LSA's regional sessions, for example, modeled or demonstrated the interactions occurring in productive professional learning communities and processes associated with collaborative inquiry.

As a second form of influence on the informal learning of its members, LSA served as a PD "catalyst" primarily by identifying and reinforcing the value of learning "tools" created by others in the province and elsewhere, as well as by demonstrating how those tools could be productively used. Many of these tools were government generated, and LSA's endorsement and use of them added significant legitimacy to their value for school leaders. Among the most prominent of these tools was the Ontario Leadership Framework (Chapter 3), which assumed a prominent role in LSA's theory of action. More generally, LSA's Steering Team ensured that the project's priorities were aligned with the priorities of the provincial government, as well as with districts whenever possible. This avoided most of the conflict often encountered by formal leadership programs that have internally coherent and defensible designs (e.g., Corcoran, Reilly, & Ross, 2015) but do little to acknowledge the larger district and provincial culture and policy context in which school leaders find themselves and on which most of their career rewards depend. So LSA's approach to leadership development reduced—rather than increased—the amount of buffering required of participants in order to pursue their own school improvement initiatives.

LSA as Part of a Province-Wide Strategy for the Implementation of Educational Innovations

A second perspective on LSA views it as a sustained effort to adapt and implement a large handful of innovations, as well as to encourage both knowledge transfer and utilization as a means of improving practice. An innovation is commonly understood to be a set of practices novel to a defined group of potential users and that hold promise of accomplishing a desired outcome better than the existing practices of the group. Most examples of the initiatives undertaken by LSA fitting this conception of an innovation have been about interactive processes, including the following:

- Collaborative inquiry processes often undertaken as a core feature of professional learning communities in schools. Two specific sets of inquiry procedures were advocated by the project: teaching–learning critical pathways (TLCPs) and professional learning cycles.

- TLCPs were especially aimed at the development of deep understanding of "big ideas."

- Uses of a theory of action to guide school improvement planning.

- Establishment of principal learning teams in districts.

- Knowledge building, LSA's most recent priority.

These innovations, however, have been advanced by LSA to its members as promising ideas to be worked with, further developed, and often taking different forms in different school and district contexts. This "pro-adaptive" approach (Century & Cassata, 2016, p. 199) to implementation by LSA acknowledges compelling and long-standing evidence about the need for most innovations to be adapted (Berman & McLaughlin, 1978) if they are to be successful and the need for innovation users to "make sense" of innovations in their own circumstances (Weick, 1995).

Much of LSA's work can also be conceptualized as *knowledge transfer* and *utilization*. Knowledge transfer captures much of what LSA has done to promote a focus among school leaders on the "key learning conditions," which considerable evidence suggests have a significant influence on student learning (see Chapter 6). LSA's approach to key learning conditions consisted of identifying them to members during its symposia, providing written accounts of the evidence justifying attention to the learning conditions, and including measures of the learning conditions prominently in LSA's annual evaluations. While none of the key learning conditions promoted by LSA would be considered an "innovation" by a teaching staff (e.g., time for instruction, academic emphasis, teacher trust), their relative effects on student learning were often underappreciated, as were some of the more promising approaches to enhancing these conditions in schools.

Knowledge utilization also has been central to much of the work within districts and schools that LSA has supported, for example, by encouraging the work of principal learning teams and by providing LSA district facilitators. LSA facilitators help groups of teachers and school leaders figure out how knowledge, promoted as relevant in LSA forums and through other avenues, can be useful in the context of individual schools and classrooms. These facilitators are a source of guidance for what is often primarily informal learning on the part of project members.

LSA's approach to implementing innovations and to fostering knowledge transfer and utilization demonstrates a realistic and sophisticated understanding of how local practical knowledge and knowledge from research need to be blended together if practices in schools and classrooms are to stand much chance of improving. LSA's "problems of practice" have always been defined by those responsible for solutions. But processes for solving those problems of practice have taken account of both previous research conducted in other contexts, as well as research in the Ontario provincial context. Both sources of research have been used extensively. Evidence found in research journals typically collected "somewhere else" can provide powerful sources of initial guidance. But such research often lacks local relevance or "ecological validity." Comparably rigorous research conducted locally tests the value, in participants' own contexts, of results from studies conducted "somewhere else." Mixed results reported in many reviews of research and the difficulties routinely encountered in replicating research results (e.g., Makel & Plucker, 2014; Winerman, 2013) lend credence to claims about the unique features of local contexts significantly influencing the consequences of implementing most innovative practices or making use of knowledge from somewhere else.

Some will think that arguing for the importance of conducting local research to test the ecological validity of the results of research conducted "somewhere else" raises the bar unrealistically for either professional development providers or those responsible for large-scale implementation efforts. But compare the costs of doing that local research—and finding no significant results—with the costs of either professional development or innovation implementation focused on promoting practices that turn out not to work as and where intended. It is no contest.

When such local research is not done, as is typical, the costs are almost entirely borne by those local practitioners who are often already suffering from initiative overload. Those costs to local practitioners include, for example, time wasted figuring out how to implement a new practice and the stress involved in trying to make the new practice work, as well as the money associated with training, not to mention significant opportunity costs. In contrast, when such research is done, the costs are borne by a relatively few people conducting the research as part of their job. Local research also responds to the limitations of the evidence from "somewhere else" used much of the time as justification for innovations. This evidence serves, as Chambers, Glasgow, and Stange (2013) note, to "reify early phase interventions tested in the most artificial settings" (p. 3).

LSA'S FORMAL PROFESSIONAL DEVELOPMENT PROGRAM

This section summarizes six central components of LSA's formal leadership development program and how some of those components evolved over time.

Speaker Series

The speaker series was an especially prominent part of LSA's early program. While it continues to this day, expectations for what it accomplishes have been sharply reduced and defined. Experts such as Richard Sagor, John Hattie, Andy Hargreaves, Michael Fullan, Carmel Crévola, Lorna Earl, and Steven Katz were part of the initial series, addressing such topics as emotional intelligence, action research, professional learning communities, appropriate assessment and instructional strategies, and leading schools in a data-rich world. In order to disseminate this learning at the district level, facilitators' guides and DVDs of these presentations were developed for use by participants.

Since the first year of the project, LSA has convened daylong province-wide fall and spring symposia typically attended by about four hundred project members, usually in district teams. A typical symposium begins with an introduction by members of the Steering Team; this introduction usually provides a capsule summary of the previous year's work, highlights recent priorities and progress made in their implementation, and reviews the agenda for the day. This introduction is typically followed by a major address related to a current priority and aimed at deepening members understanding of that priority and the evidence justifying attention to it. There is usually a half hour or more for attendees to discuss the content of the address among themselves in groups of six to eight and to pose questions to the speaker.

As part of the agenda, there is usually some update from a senior ministry official about the government's current educational priorities and often the state of student achievement in the province. Occasionally, the minister of education has been part of this agenda item, but most of the time it has been the assistant deputy minister responsible for student achievement in the province. Time is always provided after this item for discussion and questions.

The morning sessions typically end with an update from the project evaluator about the results of the most recent data collection and its implications for the work of both project members and the Steering Team. Following lunch, participants have a chance to attend LSA-related workshops provided by teams from participating districts and to spend time together in district teams planning the next phase of their own local work.

As this overview of a symposium indicates, time has been devoted to the introduction of innovative ideas, as well as knowledge transfer and use. The symposia have also connected LSA priorities with Ministry of Education initiatives helping members appreciate the coherence of improvement work undertaken across the province with efforts in their own schools and districts. An increasingly important component of these symposia also has been time provided for district teams to plan together, as well as breakout workshops provided by district teams to any symposia participants with an interest in similar problems of practice.

The design of these provincial symposia needs to be understood in the context of LSA's overall program. The provincial symposia serve as a primary source of information about future directions and progress with existing directions, whereas other components of the program emphasize knowledge use and capacity building in members' schools.

District Leaders' Symposia

LSA has provided central office leaders responsible for facilitating the LSA work of their school leaders (usually one in each district) with a separate half-day symposium the day prior to the school leader symposia. These half-day sessions foreshadow the central themes to be addressed in following days' school leaders' symposia and provide an in-depth treatment of one or more key LSA priorities, especially implications for district leadership. These half-days also provide time for central office leaders from many districts to learn more about what their colleagues from other districts are doing to enhance LSA's work in their systems.

Regional Sessions

Each year since early stages of the project, LSA has provided regional symposia with an emphasis on direct support to school staffs attempting to implement LSA priorities. During the first three years of the project, nine regional sessions were offered to the over five hundred principal team leaders and their district colleagues across the province. These symposia were videotaped and posted on the project website. DVDs with facilitator's guides were created so that principal team leaders could share their learning experiences with members of their principal learning teams, teachers, and the school community.

Workshops

During that period, the project also provided a series of one-day workshops developed by each of the three principals' associations and made them available to participating principal learning teams in their districts. These included workshops on such topics as "Implementing Professional Learning Communities," the "Ministry's School Effectiveness Framework," "Leadership for Literacy," "Leading in Math," "Data Driven Decision Making," and "Principal Action Research."

Web conferences (online workshops) were a popular addition in the third year. Principal learning teams were also provided with articles and books that supported the goals of the project. In addition, the Ministry of Education's Literacy and Numeracy Secretariat also made available "student achievement officers" (very knowledgeable consultants) to work with teachers in schools on developing specific strategies to raise student achievement in literacy and numeracy.

Interactive Technologies

Through its contract with Learnography, LSA resources have included such interactive technologies as the LSA websites, the LSA Web network, and a series of virtual learning programs or webinars. The LSA English and French websites are warehouses of resources. They contain records of webcasts, details of the LSA project, and the LSA theory of action. Revisions to the websites have included updated URLs, a new home page (in process), and an interactive version of LSA theory of action, along with "How-To Guides" providing step-by-step instructions for using the LSA networks.

The LSA Web networks are places to continue conversations; they provide the opportunity to share experiences, resources, and knowledge. At one point, these networks had approximately 3,500 members, two hundred videos, one hundred discussion forums, and seventy groups.

The use of digital technology to improve the quality of leadership development experiences, as well as to improve access to those experiences, has been widely assumed to have high potential. LSA's early experience with quite high-quality technology demonstrated its uses but also revealed some important challenges. Admittedly, one of the challenges experienced at earlier points in the project, consistent use, would not exist now simply because such technology is now much more ubiquitous.

A series of phone interviews was conducted in February 2010 with fourteen principals who self-identified in advance as users of LSA's web-based resources and opportunities.[1] Questions asked of these principals were about how the web-based materials were being used, what was the extent and impact of such use, challenges encountered, and suggestions for improving the LSA's website. Only a very small proportion of LSA members were actually making anything like regular use of the website and Ning. Much of that use was as a consequence of its demonstrations at LSA symposia. The most frequent use was prompted by a group, led by two members of the ministry's student achievement secretariat, titled "Working Together Really Matters."

More generally and as intended, the website was viewed at that time by those small numbers of principals using it as an important resource for their own professional learning, as well as the learning of their staffs. The highest degree of reported activity was in the video section of the LSA Ning, followed by activity on the web conferences and group sections of the Ning.

Several interview respondents claimed a direct impact on student learning of what teachers were learning through their web and collaborative inquiry experiences. But most of the reported impacts were on teachers' work alone resulting from, for example, access to models of especially effective instruction and other useful ideas, expanding the network of colleagues for teachers, and seeing new possibilities for the use of technology for instruction.

Lack of time to become familiar with and explore web material was the most frequently cited challenge. However, respondents also identified some awkward features of the website and challenges with their own school's technology for making collaborative use of web resources. Users of the website spoke about a lack of awareness of the site among their colleagues. More communication about the website would be worthwhile, they suggested. Such communication should be designed to increase awareness of the site to those not currently using it or not using it regularly. Interviewees also suggested that the website could benefit from some reorganization, especially the "Video Section," which could use an index or framework to make it easier and faster to find

---

[1] There was no overlap in the two samples of principals who were interviewed.

what you were looking for. And some principals could use more basic training in website use.

Results of the interviews suggested that the LSA website and Ning were being used by a very small proportion of project members on a regular basis. Those using it found it worthwhile, especially to support their own professional learning activities and those of their staffs.

Implications of the interview results led to the recommendation that the structure and content of the website continue to be refined in response to the suggestions of those using it. The LSA website, interview evidence suggested, held considerable potential for both deepening and expanding project work. It had the potential, some believed, to become the most visible face of the project in the future, although five years later, this outcome seems to have been overly optimistic. So the Steering Team was encouraged to explore ways in which to make use of the website routine for almost all LSA participants.

LSA Facilitators

Two types of external expertise have been available to project participants: LSA facilitators and student achievement officers. Both sources of expertise support LSA members, sometimes individually and sometimes in teams, to adapt LSA priorities to the unique contexts of their organization and to foster knowledge use. LSA facilitators are also members of the LSA Steering Team, and most have been associated with the project and its evolving priorities for many years.

The ministry's student achievement officers, chosen for their instructional leadership abilities, work closely with the LSA project. Results from the LSA evaluation have found them to be highly valued as a source of assistance by the vast majority of those providing data while a few were unaware of either the existence or the name of the officer assigned responsibility for their school. Some inferred that there might be such an officer but that this person might be working more directly with senior staff, while others vaguely recalled having met the officer but could not remember specifically who this person was.

Student achievement officers represented a valuable source of expertise for districts and schools in their efforts to improve math and language achievement. The selection criteria for these positions included significant administrative experience, along with deep pedagogical content knowledge. Access to them by LSA members was possible because of the symbiotic relationship between the provincial ministry of education and the LSA project. Without that relationship, this extraordinary resource would be out of the reach of LSA to provide by itself.

CONCLUSION

As this chapter has made clear, LSA's approach to large-scale leadership development has been both dynamic and complex. Its dynamic nature is rooted in commitments to evidence-informed decision making about project directions, in combination with strong and widely shared norms among project leaders to persist and improve rather than abandon initiatives that did not immediately demonstrate the outcomes for which they were designed. Efforts made to ensure alignment of project priorities with those of the provincial government have reduced the need for project members to be buffered from competing demands for change. This has not meant that LSA's priorities are always determined by government priorities. There are significant instances of the reverse, as well as the identification of initiatives and priorities that lie outside but do not conflict with current government priorities.

Chapter 5

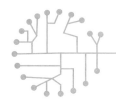

COLLABORATIVE INQUIRY

From the outset, the LSA project has encouraged its members to approach their school improvement efforts using some form of collaborative inquiry. But there has been considerable evolution, over the life of the project, in LSA's understanding about how such inquiry can best be fostered. This evolving understanding has largely been promoted by results from the project's annual evaluations. With collaborative inquiry as the focus, this chapter illustrates especially clearly how the LSA project "learned its way forward" with most of the practices it has sponsored and supported.

Before describing LSA's evolving approaches to collaborative inquiry, however, it is important to appreciate why collaborative inquiry emerged as and remains central to the project's commitments, whatever their form. The explanation is a largely implicit but nonetheless unwavering belief in what learning scientists refer to more formally as situated and social constructivist perspectives on learning (e.g., Murphy & Knight, 2016). From a social constructivist perspective, authentic learning is strongly influenced by the context in which it takes place and is directed by the learner's own interests. Learning by individuals occurs as part of the activity in which those individuals are engaged and is prompted by interactions with others engaged in similar activity. Situated cognition extends this perspective by acknowledging the context as an especially central influence on what is learned. These views of learning subsume most features attributed to informal learning (Kindt, Gijbels, Grosemans, & Donch, 2016; Rogoff, Callanan, Gutierrez, & Erickson, 2016) as it was described in Chapter 3.

A deeply held belief in situated and social constructivist perspectives on learning also helps to explain the "pro-adaptive" assumptions made by project leaders about the types of help members would need to successfully implement the series of new practices or "innovations" that have accumulated over time as part of LSA's portfolio. While an innovation may arrive with substantial evidence of its value, making the innovation work in the unique situations found in each members' schools would require adaptations best developed through collaborative inquiry among those intended to use it.

Informal but extensive evidence suggests that implicit situated and social constructivist beliefs held by LSA project leaders' parallel beliefs about learning held by many of the project's school leaders and their teachers, although the implications of those beliefs are not always reflected in their schools' actual classroom instruction. LSA's efforts to foster collaborative inquiry, however, have been closely aligned with the instructional implications of situated and social constructivist theory (Rogoff et al., 2016): these efforts have been successful to the extent that they helped members better understand how to do something they already believed in but were uncertain about how to enact.

The following account of LSA's efforts to foster productive collaborative inquiry in its members' schools, however, is not a story of easy wins. On the contrary, the project has struggled mightily to encourage the creation of structures that support collaborative inquiry and then to nurture collaborative inquiry processes that project members could use to actually improve teaching and learning in their schools. These efforts, as the chapter notes, have overlapped and intersected with other project priorities.

THE EVOLUTION OF LSA'S APPROACH TO COLLABORATIVE INQUIRY

LSA's approach to fostering collaborative inquiry began with a substantial investment in promoting principal learning teams

(PLTs) in districts and professional learning communities (PLCs) in schools. Establishing the structural features of such communities in districts and schools was the first order of business. But as evidence accumulated about weak effects and implementation challenges, attention shifted to better understanding and promoting processes and relationships within these structures that would more reliably result in instructional and school improvement. This shift in attention continues with the two main priorities of the project at the time of this writing: working with schools to implement knowledge building and conducting research on the main characteristics of effective leadership networks (PLTs).

Professional Learning Communities

Much of the attention devoted early in the project to the development of PLCs was encouraged by the widespread popularity of the PLC concept at the time, along with the extensive training materials that were developed by its advocates and champions (e.g., Dufour & Eaker, 1998). Adopted at an almost unparalleled rate across North American school systems, the concept itself was rooted in research about organizational learning, distributed cognition (Hutchins, 1995; Wenger, 1998), and evidence that associated collaborative school cultures with improved student achievement (e.g., Little, 2002; Rosenholtz, 1985). However, there was very little research reporting the contributions of PLCs to student learning at the beginning of the project. The most compelling evidence was reported by Sharon Kruse and Karen Seashore Louis (1998). PLCs were conceptualized and measured in the early years of the project after this research that defined PLCs along five dimensions, including reflective dialogue, de-privatization of practice, collective focus on student learning, collaboration, and shared norms and values. The most critical dimension in accounting for student learning, according to the Kruse and Seashore Louis research, was "de-privatization of practice."

The 2007–08 evaluation included reports of both survey and interview data concerning PLC functioning. Survey results indicated that teachers became slightly but significantly more positive about their PLCs' impact from fall to spring, but there were very small declines in the ratings of six of the nine items used to measure PLC impact. The notable exception to this pattern was teachers planning together as part of the school day. There was a large change in the rating of this item, from a very low rating in the fall to a mid-level rating in the spring, suggesting that school leaders were finding more time for collaborative inquiry by their teachers in what were then labeled PLCs.

All items measuring collaboration in creating a professional learning community increased significantly from the first to the second administration of the survey. Those items whose ratings increasing most included these: *have conversations with colleagues about school goals, have conversations with colleagues about managing classroom behavior,* and *receive meaningful feedback from colleagues about my performance.* Analyses in this year's evaluation report, using literacy and math achievement change scores, produced few significant relationships, however. One exception was a small but significant relationship between gains in Grade 6 reading and professional learning communities ($r = .19$). To put these results in perspective, however, very few published studies of educational innovations have been able to demonstrate significant effects using achievement change scores as their dependent measure.

Interview results from the same 2007–08 evaluation noted that LSA members were finding PLCs difficult to implement, as has been reported by others (e.g., Nehring & Fitzsimons, 2011; Stoll et al., 2006; Wells & Feun, 2007). PLCs entail a dramatic change in the culture of many schools, as well as the structures required in support of such change (e.g., Zang et al., 2016). Concern about time was one illustration of these difficulties. Interviewees also reported many challenges to the makeup and operation of their PLCs, in addition to finding the time that PLCs required. While some PLCs were reported to be working well, others were not so successful. For example, one PLC had become successful quite quickly, but with the loss of its coach in the third year, it had just as quickly declined in its effectiveness. Interviewees from one district reported lack of understanding among district staff about the purpose and function of PLCs; one interviewee suggested that the superintendent would be quite surprised by how ineffective the district's PLCs were. This LSA evidence mirrors a good deal of other research indicating that PLCs often fail to produce their intended effects because of poor implementation, a lack of focus, difficulties in sustaining teacher collaboration, and/or a lack of enabling structures (Hipp & Huffman, 2010; Hord & Tobia, 2012).

The evaluation report identified, as an implication of these interview results, that LSA should maintain effective PLC functioning as a priority for its continuing attention, with an emphasis on how to sustain already well-functioning PLCs. Inferences from results of the evaluation strongly suggested bringing a much sharper focus within PLCs to those conditions which the best available evidence indicates have the most powerful direct effects on student learning. This inference eventually led to an LSA focus on key learning conditions.[1]

By the following year (2009–10), survey data from the evaluation indicated that on average, while teachers were moderately positive about the impact of their professional learning communities, this variable attracted the lowest set of ratings among all those on the survey, and the ratings changed very little from fall to spring. Based on regression analysis, evaluations conducted over the three-year period from 2008–09 to 2011–12, as with results from earlier years, continued to report very weak (close to 0) effects of PLCs on student achievement in math and language.

In sum, while LSA project leaders initially anticipated that the formation of PLCs would lead to rich collaborative inquiry among teachers and school leaders and that such inquiry would stimulate significant improvements in instruction, the first two annual evaluations reported decidedly less optimistic results. These results prompted efforts to improve the functioning of PLCs, to recommend productive foci for PLC inquiry, and to situate the use of PLCs as a continuing but less prominent part of the project. The search continued for additional ways of fostering productive collaborative inquiry.

Principal Learning Teams (PLTs)

Establishing leadership networks (PLTs) within districts including all LSA members in a district was one of the first of LSA's recommendations to its members. The first interim annual evaluation report (2007–08) noted that school leaders in the project were, indeed, learning and working with one another in district-based

---

[1]See Chapter 1 for a brief definition of key learning conditions and Chapter 6 for a comprehensive treatment of LSA's approach to their use.

networks, sometimes drawing on external expertise. Most PLT members of the networks had also begun to create PLCs with their teachers in their own schools for both professional learning and school improvement purposes.

As Table 5.1 indicates, four items were included in the scale measuring characteristics of PLTs. Two of these items measured PLT members' knowledge and skill, and two measured PLT members' dispositions. The mean response to all items in the scale was in the "agree to strongly agree" range in both the fall and spring ($\mu = 4.14$ and 4.13, respectively, on a 5-point scale). The response pattern for these items was the same on both occasions, with lower ratings in the spring. None of the rating decreases were statistically significant, however. The two lowest-rated items concerned the knowledge and skill of PLT members. Lowest rated (but still at the upper end of the agree response) of the four items was "Most members of our PLT have the knowledge and skill they need to improve students' literacy and mathematics learning" ($\mu = 3.85$ and 3.93 on the 5-point scale). "Members of our PLT exude a belief in the capacity of their teachers to help even the most difficult children achieve high standards in literacy and math" ($\mu = 3.99$ and 3.98) was the second-lowest-rated item.

The two highest-rated items were about attitudes or dispositions, as distinct from knowledge and skills. "In our PLT, continuous improvement in literacy and math achievement is viewed by most members as a necessary part of the job in their schools" ($\mu = 4.45$ and 4.42) was the highest-rated item, followed by "In our PLT instructional improvement problems are viewed as issues to be solved not as barriers to action" ($\mu = 4.27$ and 4.19).

Three items asked participants to judge the value to the development of their own leadership of PLT participation. The mean response to the items in this scale was 4.40 in the fall; principals agreed to strongly agreed that their PLT participation was making a valuable contribution to their individual leadership. Spring ratings were significantly lower, however. Participation in a PLT was rated a bit more beneficial ($\mu = 4.59$ and 4.42) than was being a leader of a PLT ($\mu = 4.23$ and 4.09) on both occasions. Principals agreed to strongly agreed that PLT participation had improved their instructional leadership capacities ($\mu = 4.34$), a belief that was weaker in the spring ($\mu = 4.22$).

TABLE 5.1 LSA Members' Ratings of PLT Characteristics and Value[2]

PLT CHARACTERISTICS AND VALUE	FALL			SPRING			CHANGE
	N	MEAN	SD	N	MEAN	SD	
PLT Characteristics Aggregate	551	4.14	.59	746	4.13	.60	.79
1. Members have knowledge and skill	559	3.85	.83	748	3.93	.78	
2. Continuous improvement viewed necessary	555	4.45	.69	746	4.42	.73	
3. Instructional improvement problems as solvable	552	4.27	.74	742	4.19	.75	
4. Belief in teachers' capacity to help difficult students	547	3.99	.78	743	3.98	.77	
Value of PLT Participation Aggregate	541	4.40	.67	731	4.25	.78	.83
5. Participation in PLT beneficial to me	541	4.59	.68	728	4.42	.79	
6. Being leader of PLT beneficial to me	437	4.23	.88	542	4.09	.96	
7. PLT improved my instructional leadership	537	4.34	.78	735	4.22	.87	

These results were interpreted by the LSA Steering Team as further support for developing principals' and teachers' knowledge and skill for improving literacy and math achievement. The dispositions necessary to motivate such improvement seemed to be extremely well developed, at least from the perspective of principals.

Results from the following year's evaluation (2009–10) found that participants generally rated items measuring their PLTs very high in relation to most other variables measured by the survey. At the beginning of the year, the highest of these ratings was awarded to the disposition or attitude, within their PLTs, about the necessity of continuous improvement, followed by instructional improvement

[2]A 5-point rating scale used; 1 = not at all, 5 = to a great extent.

PLT = principal learning team; N = number of respondents; SD = standard deviation.

as a solvable problem. Respondents were more circumspect about the knowledge and skills of their PLT colleagues. Unlike the previous year's pattern, these ratings improved slightly over the year rather than declining.

The significant value LSA members awarded to their early experiences with membership in a leadership network or PLT has persisted over the dozen years of the project's duration. Both the 2015 and 2016 evaluations requested members rate the value of twelve potential sources of their professional learning. The results both years were almost exactly the same and appear in Table 5.2. As these data indicate, participation in PLTs was rated second in value only to personal professional reading. Because LSA members have consistently viewed collaborative inquiry in their PLTs as contributing most to their own development, LSA has recently made improving the functioning of PLTs one of its two key priorities for work in the near future. The nature of this work is described more fully in Chapter 8.

Teaching–Learning Critical Pathways (TLCPs) 2009–10

In addition to maintaining its focus on key learning conditions in elementary schools (academic press; disciplinary climate; collective teacher efficacy; teachers' trust in colleagues, parents, and students; and uses of instructional time), the phase of work evaluated over the 2009–10 project year continued to support the implementation and refinement of a collaborative process called *teaching–learning critical pathways* (TLCPs). This approach to collaborative work in schools aimed at engaging staff in improving instruction concerned, in particular, with those complex concepts, ideas, and skills in the Ontario provincial curriculum. As well, the 2009–10 phase of LSA's efforts extended the project into at least several secondary schools in each of twelve of Ontario's seventy-two districts and both refined and extended its web presence among project participants.

The most detailed description of a TLCP was captured by the survey items used, in the quantitative portion of the project's evaluation, to measure the extent of TLCP implementation. According to these items, the TLCP process encouraged collaboration among teachers for the purpose of planning lessons and units of instruction, as

TABLE 5.2 Value Attributed by School Leaders to Potential Sources of Their Own Learning[3]

SOURCES OF SCHOOL LEADERS' LEARNING	N	MEAN	SD
Aggregate response	**395**	**2.66**	**.49**
A central office leader (e.g., SO, system principal, SEF lead, leadership lead) with close knowledge of my school	399	2.88	.96
Another central office leader not directly responsible for my school	394	2.49	.97
One or more of my own staff members	397	2.88	.89
Scheduled PD sessions provided by my district	396	2.76	.81
PD opportunities provided by LSA (e.g., symposia, regional sessions, virtual sessions, LSA Web)	396	2.56	.95
Sessions facilitated by Student Achievement Division (e.g., Literacy and Numeracy Secretariat, Student Success: Learning to 18, Leadership)	394	2.50	.91
My Principal Learning Team	392	*3.01*	.86
Other networks in which I participate	392	2.78	.93
My professional reading (print and online)	396	*3.15*	.75
University-sponsored program(s)	383	1.72	.93
Principal association–sponsored professional learning	390	2.49	.96

well as to decide on student assessments and how to mark student work. The TLCP process encouraged teachers, together, to choose "big ideas" as a focus for instruction and to select instructional material to assist students in understanding those big ideas. Teachers engaged in TLCPs were also expected to create explicit criteria for judging student work and to engage students in the creation and revision of those criteria (and possibly rubrics) for judging their own work. Students were to be encouraged, as part

---

[3]A 5-point rating scale used; 1 = not at all, 5 = to a great extent.

N = number of respondents; SD = standard deviation; SO = superintendent; SEF = School Effectiveness Framework leader; PD = professional development.

of the process, to provide their peers with feedback about their work based on explicit, collaboratively developed criteria.

The quantitative and qualitative data from the evaluation pointed to very different conclusions about the relative value and significance of this addition to LSAs' efforts to foster collaborative inquiry. This section begins with an overview of the main conclusions about TLCPs from the quantitative evidence and then turns to the qualitative evidence.

Quantitative Data About TLCPs

Responses to the surveys provided by elementary principals, secondary principals, department heads, and teachers, as part of the 2009–10 evaluation, pointed to moderate amounts of collaboration among school staffs for the purposes of carrying out TLCP-related processes. This evidence was interpreted as indicating considerably more room for growth in the use of TLCPs in the future, as well as the need for continuing TLCP training for principals and teachers. This call for additional training assumed that subsequent evidence would demonstrate positive effects of TLCP-related processes on student achievement. In fact, when such evidence became available, TLCP effects on student learning were, at best, weak. But the quantitative portion of the evaluation noted that all the key learning conditions had significant effects on student learning, and implemented with integrity, TLCP processes potentially created environments and dispositions congenial to the further development of key learning conditions.

The quantitative portion of the following year's evaluation (2010–11) concluded that the relatively low overall value awarded by teachers to their involvement in TLCP processes for student learning and the moderate rating they assigned to the helpfulness of TLCP training was likely the most striking result of that year's evaluation. The generally upbeat, positive, even enthusiastic tone generated by teachers in the TLCP training sessions was not reflected in the numerical and more representative data provided by the surveys. A second year's assessments of TLCP contributions to student learning also indicated weak relationships with students' math and language achievement, as compared with most of the key learning conditions.

Interviews with twenty-two principals during the early winter of 2010 provided a distinct contrast with the results of the survey results described previously. These data suggested that considerable effort was being devoted to implementing TLCP processes with a high degree of fidelity. Many respondents had received training about TLCP processes and were working through each step in the process with their staffs as it had been explained to them. Three of the more ambitious aspirations for the TLCP process were being realized, according to the interviews. First, TLCP processes were reported to be having quite positive effects on the further development of the key learning conditions. Second, participation with staff in TLCP processes was providing principals with a much better sense of what it means to provide "instructional leadership" in their schools. Third, almost all principals believed that classroom instruction in their schools had improved, sometimes dramatically, as a result of teacher participation in TLCP processes.

Interview evidence also identified three TLCP-related challenges. A lack of time for staff to develop the pathways was the most frequently cited challenge. The second challenge was the identification and development of "big ideas." A third and final challenge concerned the level of cognitive complexity required of students grappling with big ideas. The interview results shed light only indirectly on this issue, unfortunately. But increasing the cognitive complexity required of students through the instruction they receive was the core purpose for developing TLCPs. Big ideas, by themselves, were only one half of the central concept giving rise to the TLCP process; deep understanding was the other half.

In 2011, the Student Achievement Division of the Ministry of Education developed and published the professional learning cycle as a collaborative inquiry process for educators to improve student achievement and engagement. This learning cycle, an alternative to TLCPs, consisted of four steps or moves:

1. Plan—examine data to determine student need, select a learning focus, determine educator learning, and plan with the end in mind.

2. Act—implement instruction and engage in professional learning.

3. Observe—monitor student learning, share/examine evidence of student learning, and share instructional practice.

4. Reflect—examine, analyze, and evaluate results.

Once the professional learning cycle was introduced provincially, LSA made support of the cycle a priority, providing instruction at symposia and regional sessions so that participants had the opportunity to develop their knowledge and skill.

In sum, the form of collaborative inquiry represented by TLCPs—and eventually, the professional learning cycle—emerged over a three-year period as a valuable tool for some school leaders and not so much for the majority. A reasonable decision from this mixed evidence was to continue advocating either TLCPs or the professional learning cycle as a means of further developing and implementing the key school conditions, among other things, with relatively significant effects on student learning.

By themselves, these roughly comparable forms of collaborative inquiry turned out not to be the silver bullets some had hoped for. But they certainly had important uses in some schools where they became frameworks for exciting school improvement efforts. These mixed results prompted a decision by the LSA Steering Teams to build on TLCP/professional learning cycle contributions, rather than cast them aside, and to continue to support schools that found these inquiry processes useful. The two stories that appear next in this chapter illustrate just how collaborative processes were used by school leader participants in the LSA project who found these processes valuable tools for school improvement.

A Story About Collaborative Inquiry to Improve Primary Grades Reading[4]

Following its analysis of school data for June 2013 and of the provincial achievement data, staff at the Conseil scolaire catholique Franco-Nord decided to focus on primary reading for improvement using collaborative

[4]This story, translated from the original French, was written in only a slightly edited form by Crystal Côté-Poulin. Reproduced with permission.

inquiry processes. This focus was prompted by evidence over several previous years of instability in their students' reading performance. Most students were at Level 2 on the province's 4-level scale,[5] but the reasons for such performance remained a puzzle. Staff asked themselves, What happened? What wasn't working properly? What's different? Have there been any changes in our schools over the last few years? If yes, which ones?

Discussions about questions such as these gave rise to many hypotheses and confirmed the importance of improving primary students' reading as a school improvement priority. So all ten Grade 2 teachers moved forward with a collaborative inquiry aimed at improving reading. Special education teachers and school administrators were also invited to join the team. The more specific and precise question the staff posed for inquiry was, "What impact will explicitly teaching integrated comprehension strategies for the reading process have on student reading performance?" This question was based on academic research and pedagogical resources to ensure a direct link between theory and practice. It was also directly aligned with the district's improvement plan.

Implementation of the Collaborative Inquiry Model. The Grade 2 collaborative inquiry process extended from October to February. Teachers met on three occasions, two days at a time, for a total of six days. The inquiry was implemented as a "learning pathway"; this meant that teachers administered a diagnostic assessment, a formative assessment, and a summative assessment in reading within a period of about sixteen weeks. Since staff had targeted reading comprehension, each assessment was given orally. This process included elements of the province's new assessment policy (Growing Success). Students were able to identify the learning goals, to co-construct success criteria, and to accept and offer descriptive feedback, as well as to self-evaluate.

The initial inquiry meeting examined diagnostic assessments previously administered. Guided by the inquiry question, staff analyzed student results and made some assumptions and observations. Following this analysis, the district's literacy consultant worked with teachers in areas related to students' difficulties. The staff also held PLC meetings and had coteaching sessions with colleagues involved in the collaborative inquiry; classroom observations and analyses of some of the students' work were included in these coteaching sessions.

(Continued)

---

[5]Level 1 is considered equivalent to a D grade, Level 2 a C grade, and Levels 3 and 4 equivalent to B and A grades, respectively.

(Continued)

During some PLC meetings, teachers were able to meet with other staff from the primary grades to share, analyze, and discuss their students' learning. These conversations allowed teachers to reflect on students' learning while consulting their work. For each collaborative inquiry session, teachers video recorded their interviews with students. During these interviews, students recalled a text they had read and then verbally answered one explicit and one implicit question. Teachers would then note students' results on an observation scale. During the following meetings, staff analyzed proof of learning.

Reflections on the Process. During the collaborative inquiry process described earlier, students' learning remained the project's priority by using data obtained through diagnostic student reading assessments. These assessments of student needs prompted collaborative efforts to identify and implement targeted teaching strategies. Staff continued to ask, "What behaviors did the readers exhibit? What reading strategies were observed? What do the data suggest regarding the problem? What assumptions do we make regarding students and their learning? What strengths and weaknesses do the data reveal? What can we do to resolve the issue?

Staff members used triangulation of information sources (conversations, observations, products) to track students' progress in order to analyze and reflect on their observations. They engaged in "courageous conversations" among themselves, which prompted considerable reflection about their own instructional practices. The opportunity for classroom observation of colleagues was very beneficial for teachers and built confidence about their own practices. Teachers had to welcome their peers into their classrooms sometimes to coteach a lesson in front of their colleagues; this increased both levels of trust among colleagues and a willingness to take risks.

Participation of school administrators enlivened the dialogue among the staff engaged in collaborative inquiry. By providing school administrators with a better understanding of targeted teaching in reading, such participation enhanced the quality of their classroom monitoring. And finally, during PLC meetings, they were able to contribute to exchanges and ensure a follow-up to the study. These school administrators also participated in principals learning teams in order to increase their capacity with respect to monitoring, tools, and courageous conversations.

The district's literacy consultant was invited to participate in some school PLC sessions, providing pedagogical information on reading and the needs of students. Teachers also sent parents documents describing promising strategies they could apply at home to accompany them in their reading. The parents very much appreciated this.

A Story About Empowering English Language Learners (ELL) to Excel in Mathematics[6]

This story took place at St. Andrew Catholic School, a school located in the North Rexdale section of Toronto. Approximately 75 percent of the school's students come from the Middle East and speak Assyrian and/or Arabic. For many of these students, St. Andrew provides their first formal schooling experience. Approximately 20 percent of students hail from Nigeria and Ghana, and many of these students are also refugees with limited schooling. The final 5 percent of students represent a smattering of various ethnicities and cultures. The schools is a vibrant and colorful community!

Over a three-year period, St. Andrew was deeply involved in math study. From 2012 to 2014, staff engaged in math study groups composed of Grades 2–3 teachers, Grades 4–6 teachers, Grades 7–8 teachers, and a Math for Young Children Group, which included kindergarten and Grade 1 teachers. These groups engaged in deepening their own understanding of mathematical concepts in order to develop confidence among staff; teaching was carried out through problem-solving using the three-part lesson and board-writing to consolidate student learning in a collaborative and supportive environment. Some teachers reached out to the greater educational community by opening their classrooms for public research lessons and leading and facilitating sessions at several mathematics conferences. Finally, the staff engaged in coplanning and coteaching, as well as developing common assessment practices.

(Continued)

[6]This story was written by Debby Culotta and Miranda Kus, Toronto Catholic District School Board. Reproduced with permission.

(Continued)

During this collaborative inquiry, many types of improvement were evident: a renewed sense of energy and vision, along with an increase in teacher dialogue around mathematics; greater confidence among teachers with the consolidation of mathematical solutions as they became more cognizant of the big ideas underpinning the mathematical concepts taught. Students also were participating more readily in math lessons and were using mathematical terminology when explaining their thinking; they were no longer afraid to make mistakes.

Evidence from EQAO test results indicated that students were indeed making progress in their math performance. The percentage of students achieving Level 3 or more on these tests increased in Grade 3 by 12 percent, from 39 percent to 51 percent. In Grade 6, there was a 5 percent decline in the percentage of students achieving Level 3 or more (37 percent to 32 percent), but 23 percent of previous Level 1 students moved to Level 2. Perhaps the most significant evidence was provided by the school's data integration platform, which showed that none of the students who continued in the school from Grade 2 to 6 experienced a decline in their progress; these students maintained the status quo or improved their achievement.

Despite the fact that staff felt they were making a significant difference in students' math achievement, there was a gap in that accomplishment with newly arrived students who were also new to the language and new to formal education. To address this concern, during the 2014–2015 school year, the school decided to engage its ELL teachers who had not previously taken part in math study groups. The goals were to understand student readiness for learning mathematics (e.g. math content, cultural learning background, learning skills) and to become familiar with–and use–ELL learning and teaching practices in mathematics. The school also aimed to improve math content knowledge for teachers, as well as their math instructional strategies.

Math study groups continued their work but now included ELL teachers in each of the primary, junior, and intermediate sessions. The study groups wanted to know how ELL teachers could support regular classroom teachers and students through a cross-curricular approach, marrying language acquisition with mathematical concepts simultaneously. Help with these challenges came from the district's math program coordinator, Kathy Kubota-Zarivnij, as well as Dr. Richard Barwell, professor at University of Ottawa, who specialized in the ELL learner and mathematics. Dr. Barwell joined the math study groups through

Skype technology, as well as being physically present on some occasions. The collaborative inquiry began with members listening to and studying current research, provided by Dr. Barwell, about the ELL learner and mathematics. Key research findings presented to members by Dr. Barwell were as follows:

- The "myth" that mathematics transcends language is detrimental to the interests of ELL students.

- While many ELL students quickly develop a basic level of "conversational" English, it takes several years to develop more specialized "academic" English.

- Encouraging students to use their home languages in the mathematics classroom appears to be beneficial.

- Low proficiency in all languages and mathematical underachievement is clearly linked and may explain some minority groups' underperformance in mathematics. (LNS, July, 2008)

- Children can learn and be successful in mathematics in a second or additional language.

- The language of mathematics (in any language) is complex and involves more than vocabulary.

- Participating in mathematical talk is important not just for learning mathematics, but also for learning the language of mathematics.

- Bilingual students draw on many different "resources" to communicate their mathematical thinking.

- Perhaps more than any other subject, teaching and learning mathematics depends on language. Mathematics is about relationships: relationships between numbers, between categories, between geometric forms, between variables, and so on. In general, these relationships are abstract in nature and can only be brought into being through language. Even mathematical symbols must be interpreted linguistically. Thus, while mathematics is often seen as language free, in many ways learning mathematics fundamentally depends on language. For students still developing their proficiency in the language of the classroom, the challenge is considerable. Indeed, research has shown that, while many ELL students are quickly able to develop a basic level of "conversational" English, it takes several years to develop more specialized "academic" English to the same level as a native speaker. (LNS, July, 2008)

(Continued)

- Learners' home languages can play a crucial role in their learning of mathematics. Cummins suggests that students need a high degree of proficiency in at least one language in order to make satisfactory progress at school. He also proposes that students with strength in two or more languages will outperform their peers, while those without a high degree of proficiency in any language will underachieve.

Given what been had learned with Dr. Barwell's assistance, the task of the math study groups was to determine a plan of action for teachers. Collectively, these groups identified three guiding principles: as part of planning, include and address mathematical language learning goals alongside mathematics learning goals; combine language learning and mathematics learning in the same activity; and ensure students have the opportunity to talk and write mathematical language.

Key Practices at St. Andrews

- Using classroom and local community contexts for lesson problems

- Using shared reading texts (story contexts, math readers)

- Dramatization and modeling (visual models, concrete models, websites)

- Vocabulary development (oral, visual, symbolic, summary)

- Peer support (peer translators, Google translate)

- Bansho (board-writing)

- Mathematics content learning trajectory–(a) mental math across the grades and daily practice twice per day; (b) multiplication across the grades and proportional reasoning and equivalency

- Revoicing and listenership

Staff met monthly, bringing forward student artifacts, sharing strategies that were successful, and surfacing challenges experienced in the classroom. All data were collected and still reside on Google Drive accessible to all staff. Since mental math/equivalency activities were an area of focus, a school-wide survey was conducted (in November, February, and May), for all students in Grades 1–8, to measure whether the math groups' strategies were effective. All students were asked to solve the same problem: $8 + 4 = \Box + 5$

Although the same addends were used, the order and the unknown in each of the surveys were changed. In November, 19 percent of our students were able to correctly answer the question. In February, the percentage increased to 46 percent, and by May, 60 percent of the student body was able to correctly answer the problem.

Although making progress, the school staff still believed it had much work ahead of it. One of its greatest challenges was to encourage the parent community to engage in the academic "talk" around mathematics. Since the majority of the school's parents were unable to understand or speak English, a student-led learning walk (SLLW) was begun to coincide with parent/teacher interview night. Staff decided to focus on data management and probability for the first SLLW. Every staff member collected student artifacts, which were posted in the gymnasium from kindergarten through Grade 8. Each teacher posted their learning goal and curriculum expectation, as well as their success criteria, along with the student artifacts. The trajectory of learning was made explicit and very clear in this format. Students had the opportunity to walk through the gym with their teachers to talk about the math and see firsthand how each grade built onto the next. Students were then able to walk their parents through the gym on curriculum night and talk about their learning. A group of Grade 6 students were selected to escort special visitors to our school who were interested in seeing the SLLW in action. This built confidence in the student leaders, and they demonstrated considerable pride in their accomplishments.

As the school moved toward its next academic year, it planned to continue with the math study groups, inclusive of our ELL teachers and in a collaborative and supportive environment, plan and implement strategies that work best in our ELL population. Staff believe that all of the school's students can achieve success and will continue to work to ensure that they do.

CONCLUSION

The introduction to this chapter asserted that the LSA project had struggled mightily to encourage the creation of structures that support collaborative inquiry and then to nurture development of collaborative inquiry processes that project members could use to improve teaching and learning in their schools. At many points in time, the project Steering Team could have decided to give up on collaborative inquiry, and they could have pointed to good evidence in support of that decision. But the two school stories, one about improving reading and the other about improving math, illustrate the value of collaborative inquiry processes in school contexts populated by teachers and principals disposed to develop and use such processes. These processes, as the two stories indicate, were embedded in structures (e.g., PLCs, study groups) that quantitative evidence from the LSA evaluation found to have few payoffs for students. Clearly, what goes on inside these structures is far more important than the structures themselves. The structures simply open up possibilities, but it is the interactions that occur as a result of those possibilities that matter most.

This understanding has led project leaders to establish, as project priorities, three significantly more sophisticated approaches to extending the effects of collaborative inquiry: extended research on the processes that occur inside effective leadership networks (Chapter 8), implementation of an inquiry approach to classroom instruction known as knowledge building (Chapter 9), and, beginning in 2017, the creation of several networked improvement communities (see Bryk, Gomez, & Grunow, 2011, for a brief description).

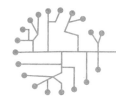

Chapter 6

KEY LEARNING CONDITIONS

A Subject for Collaborative Inquiry

Chapter 5 described LSA's early efforts to help project members develop structures and processes in support of collaborative inquiry in their schools. As that chapter also indicated, the implementation of these structures and processes made positive but, overall, modest contributions to improving teaching and learning in members' schools.

Consistent with LSA's commitment to evidence-informed decision making, results of the first phase of the project evaluation quite directly informed deliberations among members of the project Steering Team about what could be done over the next several years that would take the project to the next level. This chapter briefly describes the basis for continuing to prioritize two existing priorities (professional learning communities [PLCs] and classroom instruction) and summarizes the evidence that persuaded LSA to adopt a focus on what the project referred to as key learning conditions. These continuing and new priorities were identified in a position paper developed for the LSA Steering Team.[1]

The position paper began by identifying two existing priorities (PLCs and classroom instruction) that evidence suggested should

---

[1]The chapter is based on that position paper (Leithwood, 2007).

be continued; both conform to the qualities associated with the meaning of key learning conditions described in the remainder of this chapter. One of these existing priorities was the continuing development of PLCs within and across schools in support of collaborative inquiry and the improvement of instruction in literacy and mathematics. At the time, it was assumed that PLCs had the potential to provide both the structure and the stimulus for instructional improvement in many schools once the inquiry processes within PLCs became more effective. The second existing priority recommended for continuation was classroom instruction. Chapter 9 provides a fuller explanation of LSA's continuing efforts to improve instruction.

KEY LEARNING CONDITIONS

Leadership influence had been conceptualized from the beginning of the project as having an indirect influence on student learning. Such influence was understood to be mediated by conditions in schools and classrooms. The primary objective of the position paper developed to help identify new priorities was to follow through on that conception by taking the next obvious step: explicitly identifying a manageable number of school and classroom conditions (in addition to PLCs and focused instruction) that considerable amounts of high-quality evidence indicated (a) had significant effects on student learning and (b) could be influenced by leadership practices. It was the exercise of influence on the further development of these key learning conditions that became LSA's more precise meaning of "instructional leadership" for the project. This conception of instructional leadership mirrors many of the features now associated with learning-centered leadership (LCL). As Goff, Goldring, Guthrie, and Bickman (2014) explain,

> the term LCL has expanded upon the notion of instructional leadership. LCL includes aspects of school leadership that go beyond the instructional program of the school and highlight the importance of the focus of principals' actions on supporting teachers to improve instruction, focusing school goals on high standards and a rigorous curriculum, allocating resources aligned with teaching and learning, and developing commitment to shape the organizational culture. (p. 686)

The largest proportion of LSA's position paper was a relatively comprehensive review of empirical evidence about powerful but malleable school and classroom conditions, in addition to PLCs and focused instruction. Results pointed to five key learning conditions, including academic press or emphasis, disciplinary climate, collective teacher efficacy, teacher trust in others, and uses of instructional time.

Aside from their powerful direct effects on student learning, the paper pointed out that these five conditions have two other qualities in common. They are properties of the group, and they are "soft"—sociopsychological—states rather than bricks and mortar, money, contracts, or teaching materials. Both of these qualities make them quintessentially suitable for the attention of school-level leaders. Those leaders physically in the school can act, often within their PLCs, in ways that are more sensitive to the underlying beliefs, values, and emotions from which these conditions spring. Furthermore, there is little dependence on resources controlled largely outside the school in order to nurture the development of these school conditions.

The remainder of this chapter summarizes the evidence reviewed in the position paper that persuaded LSA's Steering Team to award priority to each of the five key learning conditions. This evidence was used, as well, to help persuade project members to nurture the development of the five conditions in their schools.

INITIAL JUSTIFICATION FOR FIVE KEY LEARNING CONDITIONS

Academic Press or Emphasis (AP)

In schools with academic press, administrators and teachers set high but achievable school goals and classroom academic standards. They believe in the capacity of their students to achieve and encourage their students to respect and pursue academic success. School administrators supply resources, provide structures, and exert leadership influence. Teachers make appropriately challenging academic demands and provide quality instruction to attain these goals. Students value these goals, respond positively, and work hard to meet the challenge.

Research on effective schools identified academic press as one important correlate of effective school climate and linked it with student achievement as early as the late 1970s and early 1980s (e.g., Hallinger, 1981; Murphy, Weil, Hallinger, & Mitman, 1982). Of the more than twenty empirical studies of academic press that have been published since about 1989, by far the majority have reported significant, positive, though moderate, relationships between academic press and student achievement, most often in the area of math, but extending to other subjects such as writing, science, reading, and language, as well. Academic press is described as explaining almost 50 percent of the between-school variability in mathematics and reading in Goddard, Hoy, and Hoy's (2000) study, for example, after controlling for the effects of students' family backgrounds. Most of the evidence suggests that a school's academic press makes an especially valuable contribution to the achievement of disadvantaged children.

Academic press is one of the more malleable conditions for leadership intervention, and a small number of studies have provided some guidance on the practices likely to increase a school's academic press (e.g. Alig-Mielcarek, 2003; Jacob, 2004). Included among those practices are the following:

- Promoting school-wide professional development
- Monitoring and providing feedback on the teaching and learning processes
- Developing and communicating shared goals
- Being open, supportive, and friendly
- Establishing high expectations
- Not burdening teachers with bureaucratic tasks and busy work
- Helping to clarify shared goals about academic achievement
- Grouping students using methods that convey academic expectations
- Protecting instructional time
- Providing an orderly environment
- Establishing clear homework policies

- Monitoring student performance in relation to instructional objectives

- Base remediation efforts on the common instructional framework

- Requiring student progress reports to be sent to the parents

- Making promotion dependent on student mastery of basic grade-level skills

Evidence about the contributions of academic press or emphasis to student achievement has continued to accumulate since LSA adopted this school condition as one of its priorities (e.g., Malloy & Leithwood, 2017).

School Disciplinary Climate

In the last couple of decades, there has been a shift in the focus of research on discipline from individual students to the school. Ma and Willms (2004) argue that the traditional way of dealing with indiscipline, mainly at the classroom level, seems insufficient and that the disciplinary climate of the classroom and school has important effects on students. This climate is shaped by features of schools and the larger community. For example, classroom disruption can be a direct reflection of the conflict or tension between teachers and students across the school, as a whole.

Using a comprehensive U.S. database, Ma and Willms (2004) developed a multidimensional conception of school disciplinary climate covering "student discipline perceptions and experiences, school culture, teacher classroom management, student engagement and commitment, school prevention and intervention in response to indiscipline, and conflicts in the social and cultural values between schools and students" (p. 10). Incorporating similar work by others, the dimensions of disciplinary climate include the following:

- Students' discipline concerns (e.g., drug use, physical conflicts)

- Class disruptions (e.g., students disrupt class, noise and disorder in class)

- Student absenteeism and tardiness

- Students' counseling about discipline

- Students' discipline experience (student had something stolen)
- The rules for behavior
- Race or cultural conflicts at the school
- Students' behaviors and the punishments for misbehaviors at the school
- Teachers' behavior (e.g., absenteeism)
- Teacher–student relations (e.g., students get along with teachers, fairness of discipline)

Research during the last decade, in particular, has produced consistent evidence demonstrating the contribution of a school's disciplinary climate to the learning of its students. Importantly, a large proportion of this research has used very large data sets and sophisticated statistical methods (in particular, hierarchical linear modeling). By way of illustration, Ma and Klinger (2000) studied the entire Grade 6 student population in 148 schools in Alberta. Their results indicated that disciplinary climate and academic press both had significant absolute effects in mathematics, science, and writing. These effects were over and above the effects of selected student variables and average school socioeconomic status; disciplinary climate was the most important determinant of academic achievement in this study.

Existing research offers very limited guidance about what leaders might do to develop the disciplinary climate in their schools. What evidence there is (e.g., Benda, 2000; Leithwood, Louis, Anderson, & Wahlstrom, 2004) recommends flexible rather than rigid responses by leaders to disciplinary events and engagement of staff and other stakeholders in developing school-wide behavior plans. A broader body of evidence does indicate that "the principal is the most potent factor in determining school climate" and that "a direct relationship between visionary leadership and school climate and culture is imperative to support teacher efforts that lead to the success of the instructional [and disciplinary] program" (Benda, 2000, p. 97). Clearly, near-term insights about the further development of this condition in schools will need to come from the collective wisdom of one's colleagues and active experimentation in one's school.

Evidence about the contributions of disciplinary climate to student achievement has continued to accumulate since LSA adopted this school condition as one of its priorities (e.g., Wu, Hoy, & Tarter, 2013).

Collective Teacher Efficacy (CTE)

Collective teacher efficacy is the level of confidence a group of teachers feels about its ability to organize and implement whatever educational initiatives are required for students to reach high standards of achievement. The effects of efficacy or collective confidence on performance is indirect through the persistence it engenders in the face of initial failure and the opportunities it creates for a confident group to learn its way forward (rather than giving up).

In highly efficacious schools, evidence suggests that teachers accept responsibility for their students' learning. Learning difficulties are not assumed to be an inevitable by-product of low socioeconomic status, a lack of ability, or family background. CTE creates high expectations for students, as well as the collectively confident teachers. Evidence suggests that high levels of CTE encourage teachers to set challenging benchmarks for themselves, engage in high levels of planning and organization, and devote more classroom time to academic learning. High CTE teachers are more likely to engage in activity-based learning, student-centered learning, and interactive instruction. Among other exemplary practices, high CTE is associated with teachers adopting a humanistic approach to student management, testing new instructional methods to meet the learning needs of their students, providing extra help to students who have difficulty and displaying persistence and resiliency in such cases, rewarding students for their achievements, believing their students can reach high academic goals, displaying more enthusiasm for teaching, committing to community partnerships, and having more ownership in school decisions.

While the total number of well-designed studies inquiring about CTE effects on students was still modest, results were both consistent and impressive. This relatively recent evidence demonstrates a significant positive relationship between collective teacher efficacy and achievement by students in such areas of the curriculum as reading, math, and writing. Furthermore—and perhaps more surprising—several of the studies have found that the effects on achievement of CTE exceed the effects of students socioeconomic status (e.g., Goddard et al., 2000), a variable that typically explains, by far, the bulk of achievement variation across schools, usually in excess of 50 percent. High CTE schools also are associated with lower suspension and dropout rates, as well as greater school orderliness (Tschannen-Moran & Barr, 2004).

There are two sources of insight about how leaders might improve the collective efficacy of their teaching colleagues. One source is the theoretical work of Albert Bandura (1993), clearly the major figure in thinking about CTE. His work, by now widely supported empirically, identifies a number of conditions that influence the collective efficacy of a group: opportunities to master the skills needed to do whatever the job entails, vicarious experiences of others performing the job well, and beliefs about how supportive the setting is in which one is working. Leaders have the potential to influence all of these conditions, for example, by doing the following:

- sponsoring meaningful professional development,

- encouraging their staffs to network with others facing similar challenges in order to learn from their experiences, and

- structuring their schools to allow for collaborative work among staff.

A second source of insight about how leaders might improve the collective efficacy of their teaching colleagues is the small number of studies that have inquired directly about the leadership practices that improve CTE. For the most part, these have been studies of transformational leadership practices on the part of principals. Evidence from these studies demonstrates significant positive effects on CTE when principals do the following:

- clarify goals by, for example, identifying new opportunities for the school, developing (often collaboratively), articulating, and inspiring others with a vision of the future, promoting cooperation and collaboration among staff toward common goals;

- offer individualized support by, for example, showing respect for individual members of the staff, demonstrating concern about their personal feelings and needs, maintaining an open-door policy, and valuing staff opinions; and

- provide appropriate models of both desired practices and appropriate values ("walking the talk").

Evidence about the contributions of collective teacher efficacy to student achievement has continued to accumulate since LSA adopted this school condition as one of its priorities. Donohoo (2017), for example, provides a recent review of this evidence.

Teacher Trust

Trust is conceptualized in many different specific ways. But almost all efforts to clarify the nature of trust include a belief or expectation, in this case on the part of most teachers, that their colleagues, students, and parents support the school's goals for student learning and will reliably work toward achieving those goals. Transparency, competence, benevolence, and reliability are among the qualities persuading others that a person is trustworthy.

Teacher trust is critical to the success of schools, and nurturing trusting relationships with students and parents is a key element in improving student learning (e.g., Lee & Smith, 1999). Dimensions of trust shown to be related to positive outcomes in school include these:

- Benevolence: a person's confidence that his or her well-being and/or things he or she holds dear will not be harmed

- Reliability: a person's belief that individuals will act consistently in ways that are beneficial those who commit their trust

- Competence: beliefs in the ability of a person to perform consistently and up to a well-known standard

- Honesty: including beliefs about a person's truthfulness, integrity, and authenticity

- Openness

Trust remains a strong predictor of student achievement even after the effects of student background, prior achievement, race, and gender have been taken into account in some recent studies of trust in schools. Goddard (2003) argues that when teacher–parent, and teacher–student relationships are characterized by trust, academically supportive norms and social relations have the potential to move students toward academic success. Results of a second study by Goddard, Tschannen-Moran, and Hoy (2001) provide one of the largest estimates of trust effects on student learning. In this study, trust explained 81 percent of the variation between schools in students' math and reading achievement.

Principal leadership has been highlighted in recent evidence as a critical contributor to trust among teachers, parents, and students (e.g., Bryk & Schneider, 2003). This evidence suggests that principals engender trust with and among staff and with both parents and students when they do the following:

- recognize and acknowledge the vulnerabilities of their staff;
- listen to the personal needs of staff members and assist as much as possible to reconcile those needs with a clear vision for the school;
- create a space for parents in the school and demonstrate to parents that they (principal) are reliable, open, and scrupulously honest in their interactions;
- buffer teachers from unreasonable demands from the policy environment or from the parents and the wider community;
- behave toward teachers in a friendly, supportive, and open manner; and
- set high standards for students and then follow through with support for teachers.

Evidence about the contributions of teacher trust in others to student achievement has continued to accumulate since LSA adopted this school condition as one of its priorities (e.g., Forsyth, Adams, & Hoy, 2011).

Uses of Instructional Time

Time spent learning is an obvious although often overlooked condition with substantial effects on student achievement. In schools that recognize the importance of how students spend their time, school schedules, timetables, structures, administrative behaviors, instructional practices, and the like are all designed to ensure that students are engaged in meaningful learning for as much of their time in school as possible. Distractions from meaningful learning are minimized. Students are academically engaged most of their time in school.

Early research on time for learning introduced several distinctions within the concept of school learning time. The broadest such conception, the total amount of time potentially available for learning, is a simple function of the number of days of schooling per year and the number of hours of instruction per day. Research often using student attendance data as an independent measure has assessed the effects of this concept of learning time on student achievement. Several other, more precise concepts of time for learning have also been the subject of research:

- Time actually devoted to instruction: this is the potential time left for learning once unplanned events, recesses, transitions, interruptions, and the like are subtracted from the total potential time;

- Opportunity to learn (OTL): this is a targeted version of time actually devoted to instruction acknowledging that the content or focus of time devoted to instruction has significant effects on the nature of student learning. This time-related concept was first introduced by Carroll (1963) in his model of school learning. Carroll's model assumes that if every student were given the necessary amount of classroom instruction time needed, relative to their individual aptitude, each would have the opportunity to succeed.

- Academically engaged time: this is the time students actually spend on their own learning within the time devoted to instruction.

Results of research about the effects of instructional time on student learning (e.g., Brown & Saks, 1986; Gump, 2005; Marburger, 2006; Tornroos, 2005) can be summed up as follows:

- the total amount of time potentially available for instruction, typically measured as student attendance rates, has been reported to have effects on student learning varying from weakly significant to quite strong;

- the total amount of time actually spent on instruction has moderate effects on student learning;

- students' total amount of academically engaged time is strongly associated with student learning; and

- the content of the curriculum that students spend time studying has quite strong effects on the nature of their learning.

There has been little direct evidence reported about leadership practices for optimizing instructional time in schools, with the major exception of research on leadership "buffering." A venerable leadership practice, buffering as a contribution to organizational goals, is justified by evidence collected in both schools and many other types of organizations. In schools, buffering aims to protect the efforts of teachers from the many distractions they face from both inside and outside their organizations. Such protection allows teachers to spend their time and energies on teaching and learning.

In the case of principals, "outside" buffering entails behaviors such as running interference with unreasonable parents, supporting teachers in the discipline of students, and aligning government and district policy initiatives with the school's improvement plan (adopting initiatives that enhance the plan and ignoring those likely to move the school in a different direction). "Inside" buffering on the part of principals involves, for example, creating teaching schedules that protect time for key instructional priorities, reducing noninstructional demands on teachers during class hours, and avoiding unplanned interruptions to classes with announcements, visitors, and the like.

As well as helping to optimize the instructional uses of time in school, buffering makes significant contributions to teachers' sense of efficacy, job satisfaction, and the reduction of teachers' feelings of anxiety and stress (Leithwood, 2006). These are powerful emotions with significant effects on the quality of teachers' instruction and their contributions to students' learning.

Evidence about the contributions of uses of time for instruction to student achievement has continued to accumulate since LSA adopted this school condition as one of its priorities (e.g., Lavy, 2014).

LSA'S OWN EVIDENCE ABOUT KEY LEARNING CONDITIONS

Chapter 4 argued that setting priorities for innovation implementation on a large scale should not be done based solely on evidence from "somewhere else," that the costs of large-scale implementation are far too high for end users to rely on evidence likely to have serious challenges to its ecological validity or local relevance. In keeping with this argument, LSA's annual evaluations for five consecutive years assessed the contribution of each of the key learning conditions to achievement in math and language in project members' schools.

Results of these annual evaluations were approximately the same each year and are illustrated in Table 6.1 from the 2011 annual evaluation. This table reports effect sizes, which in this case are Pearson Correlations, of the five key learning conditions (using teacher data to measure each condition) on provincial measures of student language and math achievement. Most effect sizes in Table 6.1 are moderate and statistically significant. This is the case for the aggregate key learning conditions measures (effect sizes in the same .26 to .35 range), as well as all but uses of instructional time; evidence about this condition indicates significant relationships with all but Grade 3 reading scores, although the effect sizes are weak, especially in comparison with those reported for other key learning conditions.

The same 2011 annual evaluation reported effect sizes on student achievement for the two priorities LSA decided to continue endorsing, PLCs and focused instruction. Similar to results from other years, neither of these learning conditions contributed much to student achievement. Effect sizes for PLCs were .01 for math achievement and −.03 for language achievement. In the case of focused instruction, effect sizes on language achievement were .17 and on math achievement .13. Subsequent evidence, however, indicated that although PLCs could not be linked directly to student achievement, they did seem to assist in the development of the five key learning conditions, a plausible function of PLCs.

TABLE 6.1 Effect Size of the Relationships Between Key Learning Conditions and Student Achievement

(Grade 3, N = 176 schools; Grade 6, N = 162 schools)

	GRADE 3				GRADE 6				BOTH
	READING	WRITING	MATH	MEAN	READING	WRITING	MATH	MEAN	MEAN
Learning Conditions Aggregate	.26**	.31**	.32**	.32**	.34**	.31**	.32**	.34**	.35**
Academic Press	.21**	.25**	.23**	.25**	.29**	.32**	.31**	.33**	.32**
Disciplinary Climate	.33**	.37**	.41**	.40**	.37**	.38**	.38**	.40**	.43**
Collect Teacher Efficacy	.20**	.24**	.24**	.24**	.33**	.31**	.33**	.35**	.30**
Teacher Trust Others	.39**	.40**	.40**	.42**	.32**	.30**	.35**	.35**	.41**
Uses of Instruction Time	.09	.16*	.17*	.15*	.23**	.23**	.15	.21**	.19**

*significant at the .05 level
**significant at the .01 level

CONCLUSION

What LSA's own evidence still has not done, however, is to provide evidence justifying a continuing focus on focused instruction.
Grappling with the identification of approaches to instruction that
can be included among LSA priorities remains a challenge for the
project. So the project's priorities continue to evolve at least significantly in response to its own evaluations. Chapters 8 describes
work undertaken to provide principal learning teams with better
guidance on how to maximize their efforts. Chapter 9 describes the
knowledge building approach, replacing focused instruction, that
LSA is now placing large bets on. Nonetheless, five annual rounds of
evidence have made a compelling case for continuing to encourage
attention to the key learning conditions described in this chapter.
This justification was given a significant boost by the development
of the project's theory of action described in the next chapter.

Chapter 7

LSA'S THEORY OF ACTION AND HOW IT WAS DEVELOPED

M any of the decisions made by LSA's Steering Team since about 2009 have been guided by a formal but dynamic theory of action created from data collected as part of the project's ongoing evaluation, along with considerable evidence from the wider literatures on leadership and school change. This chapter describes how that theory of action was developed and the theory itself, as well as how one group of project members have used the theory to help guide their own school improvement efforts.

Several earlier chapters have touched on evidence about the indirect effects of school leadership on student learning (e.g., Hallinger & Heck, 1998; Leithwood & Louis, 2012; Robinson, Lloyd, & Rowe, 2008). School leadership effects are mediated by conditions in schools and classrooms that do have direct effects on student and (importantly) that can be influenced by school leaders. One of the most important contributions of LSA's theory of action was to identify those malleable "mediators" that contribute significantly to student success at school and should, therefore, be a prime focus for school leaders' improvement efforts. While the conception of leadership adopted by LSA outlined in Chapter 3 is a response to "what" good leadership consists of, LSA's theory of action addresses questions about "how" such leadership influences student learning.

HOW LSA'S THEORY OF ACTION WAS DEVELOPED

Background events and evidence leading up to the development of LSA's theory of action, touched on in previous chapters, included the LSA's Steering Team's renewed vision for the project in the summer of 2007. As part of that vision was a theory of action aimed at helping to better understand some of the project's own evaluation results. This sense-making effort was prompted especially by the inclusion in the 2008 annual evaluation of the key learning conditions, alongside other variables also measured at that time.

The 2008 annual evaluation included the formal testing of a series of models aimed at discovering the most defensible explanation of the relationship between central project initiatives about which data were available and student achievement in math and language. Some of the following descriptions of model testing and development are unavoidably technical. But it is also brief. Be patient. It won't hurt for long.

Survey data collected from project participants and their staffs measured the perceived extent to which project initiatives were being implemented. Provincial student test data were used to represent school-level achievement in math and language. Path analytic techniques[1] were used to test three models, summarized in Figures 7.1 through 7.3. These three models, accounting for a progressively larger proportion of student achievement, represent plausible and progressively more refined versions of what eventually became LSA's theory of action.

---

[1] These figures were created from a path analysis computer program called LISREL. This program "tests" the nature of the variables and relations among the variables proposed by an apriori theory, in this case, the theory of action described in the text. Given data collected about each of the variables in the theory, the program determines whether those data "fit" the theory. Various indices or statistics are used to test this fit. The models summarized in Figures 7.1 through 7.3 all fit the data according to these indices.

FIGURE 7.1   First Model

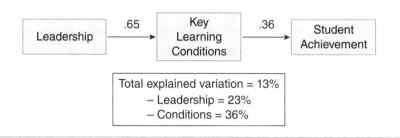

| Leadership | .65 → | Key Learning Conditions | .36 → | Student Achievement |

Total explained variation = 13%
 – Leadership = 23%
 – Conditions = 36%

Figure 7.1, the simplest model, treats the key learning conditions, along with professional learning community, as a single aggregate variable mediating the effects of leadership (as described in Chapter 3) on student learning (Grade 3 combined math and language achievement). This simple early version of a possible theory of action, as a whole, explains 13 percent of the variation in student achievement across schools, not a large amount but significant nonetheless. Of that 13 percent, leadership accounted for 23 percent, and the key learning conditions (including PLCs), in aggregate, accounted for 36 percent.

Figure 7.2, a more refined model, divided the key learning conditions, along with PLCs, into two separate sets of variables mediating leadership effects on student learning. One set, labeled "Structural Conditions," included *uses of instructional time* and *professional learning community.* The second set, labeled "Learning Conditions," included *academic press, disciplinary climate, teacher trust,* and *teacher collective efficacy.* As Figure 7.2 indicates, leadership has a relatively strong and significant direct influence on structural conditions ($r = .68$) and a weak but significant direct influence on learning conditions ($r = .25$). This model also points to a moderately significant influence of structural conditions on learning conditions ($r = .45$). Structural conditions, by themselves, however, have significant but weak and negative effects on student achievement ($r = -.21$), while learning conditions have moderately strong, positive, and significant effects on student achievement ($r = .55$).

This more refined version of LSA's theory of action explains a larger proportion of student achievement (20 percent) than the version summarized in Figure 7.1. Of this 20 percent, the indirect

FIGURE 7.2 Second Model

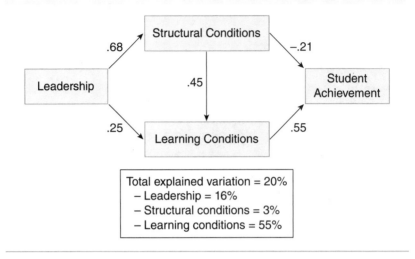

Total explained variation = 20%
— Leadership = 16%
— Structural conditions = 3%
— Learning conditions = 55%

effects of leadership account for 16 percent while the direct effects of learning conditions explain 55 percent. The direct effects of structural conditions account for an insignificant 3 percent of explained variation in student achievement. However, there was a moderately positive relationship between structural conditions and learning conditions.

The results summarized in Figure 7.2 justified separating structural variables from what was labeled "Key Learning Conditions." Clearly one set accounted for much more variation in achievement than the other. Based on these findings, the key learning conditions were subdivided into those likely to be experienced by students directly (*academic press* and *disciplinary climate*) and those likely to have less direct effects on students' experiences, *teacher efficacy* and *teacher trust*, labeled teachers' internal states in Figure 7.3.

Figure 7.3, the most complex early version of LSA's theory of action, identified three sets of variables mediating leaders' effects on student achievement. This version, as a whole, explained the largest proportion of variation in student achievement of the three versions (22 percent). Relationships between leadership and structural conditions are the same as in Figure 7.2 (*r* = .68). Also, as in

Figure 7.2, the influence of leadership on other mediators is relatively weak (.19 and .16).

Structural conditions continued to have small, significant but negative direct effects on student achievement. The direct effects of teacher internal states (*teacher efficacy* and *teacher trust*) on student achievement were essentially zero ($r = .03$) while the influence on achievement of the key learning conditions (*academic press* and *disciplinary climate*) was moderately strong, positive, and significant ($r = .53$). Figure 7.3 also shows interactions among the three sets of mediating variables, suggesting a significant positive influence of structural conditions on key learning conditions, in turn, positively influencing teacher internal states.

In Figure 7.3, leadership explains about the same proportion of student achievement as in Figure 7.2, and the scaled-down key learning conditions variable consisting of just *academic press* and *disciplinary climate* explains 55 percent. The effects of teacher internal states essentially wash out.

FIGURE 7.3 Third Model

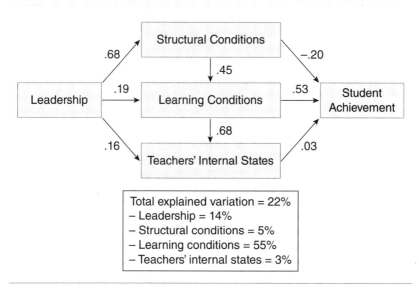

THE FOUR PATHS THEORY OF ACTION[2]

The progressive model development and testing described in Figures 7.1 through 7.3 served as a stimulus for additional conceptual work aimed at reflecting not just LSA's own evidence and existing priorities but evidence from a broader body of research, as well as current leadership theory. Results of that effort were first described in Leithwood, Anderson, Mascall, and Strauss (2010), and that version of the theory of action was then empirically tested using data from the LSA annual evaluations, along with some supplementary data (Leithwood, Patten, & Jantzi, 2010). Figure 7.4 summarizes this more fully developed theory of action, now commonly referred to as the "Four Paths Framework." The most unique feature of this framework, as compared with its earlier expressions, is the addition of the Family Path, featuring the educational culture of the home, a relatively recent LSA priority.

As Figure 7.4 indicates, LSA's initiatives are aimed at improving those leadership practices and personal leadership resources described in Chapter 3. The influence generated by such leadership "flows" along four "paths" to reach students: the Rational, Emotional, Organizational, and Family Paths. Each of these paths is populated by conditions or variables that (a) can be influenced by those exercising leadership and (b) have relatively direct effects on students. The arrow from LSA Initiatives to Leadership Practices and PLRs represents, among other things, a substantial effort by LSA to provide leaders with "domain-specific knowledge" (a personal leadership resource) about conditions in classrooms and schools that matter to student learning, as well as how to improve those conditions.

Conditions or variables on the Rational Path are rooted in the knowledge and skills of school staff members about curriculum, teaching, and learning—the technical core of schooling. The Emotional Path includes those feelings, dispositions, or affective states of staff members (both individually and collectively) shaping the nature of their work—for example, teachers' sense of efficacy. Conditions on the Organizational Path include features of schools that structure the relationships and interactions among

---

[2]Significant portions of this section are based on Leithwood, Sun, and Pollock (2017).

FIGURE 7.4 LSA Theory of Action

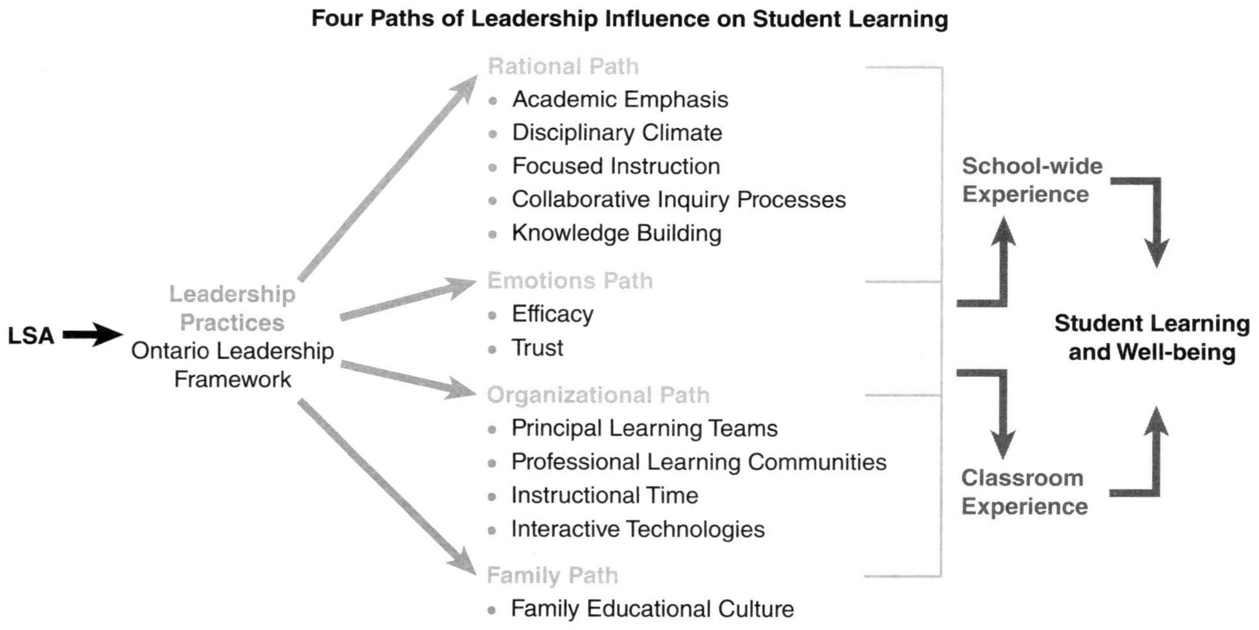

Four Paths of Leadership Influence on Student Learning

Rational Path
- Academic Emphasis
- Disciplinary Climate
- Focused Instruction
- Collaborative Inquiry Processes
- Knowledge Building

Emotions Path
- Efficacy
- Trust

Organizational Path
- Principal Learning Teams
- Professional Learning Communities
- Instructional Time
- Interactive Technologies

Family Path
- Family Educational Culture

Leadership Practices
- Ontario Leadership Framework

LSA

School-wide Experience

Student Learning and Well-being

Classroom Experience

organizational members, including, for example, cultures, policies, and standard operating procedures. On the Family Path are conditions reflecting family expectations for their children, the nature of communications between children and parents in the home, and the social and intellectual capital of parents about schooling.

Selecting the most promising of these conditions (a task requiring knowledge of relevant research, as well as local context) and improving their status are the central challenges facing leaders intending to improve student learning in their schools, according to this framework. As the status of conditions or variables on each path improves through influences from leaders and other sources, the quality of students' school and classroom experiences is enriched, resulting in greater payoffs for students. Over an extended time, leaders should attend to conditions in their schools in need of strengthening on all paths.

In sum, the job of school leaders, in collaboration with their colleagues, is to do the following:

- Identify conditions not yet sufficiently developed to realize their potential contribution on students.

- Select from those conditions, which one or several ought to become a focus for the school's improvement efforts in light of the school's current goals, priorities, and other features of the school's context.

- Generate new possibilities when current options prove insufficient.

- Plan and act to improve the status of those conditions selected for improvement.

This conception of how school leadership influences students is also an approach to school improvement, one which cedes considerable autonomy to school leaders and their colleagues about what is to be improved and how such improvement will take place. The accountability demands saturating much contemporary educational policy call for leaders who are *strategic* in making their efforts to meet the learning needs of students, to develop school conditions or cultures defined as continuous improvement, and to increase the organizational learning capacities of schools. To be strategic, school leaders need to know about those classroom, school, and malleable family conditions that both contribute significantly to student learning and that they can influence.

Approaching school improvement from the perspective described here also requires considerable "systems thinking" on the part of school leaders. While variables associated with each of the four paths are distinct, they also interact with variables on the other paths, and failure to take such interaction into account will severely limit a school leader's influence. This means, for example, that if a school leader decides to improve the status of a school's academic press (a variable on the Rational Path), she will also need to consider what her teachers' feelings will be in response. The leader will need to ensure that her teachers begin to feel, for example, efficacious about their role in fostering the school's academic press (a variable on the Emotional Path).

The need for alignment across paths seems to hugely complicate leaders' work. But, as this academic press example illustrates, picking only one or two powerful variables on a path and planning for the most likely interactions makes the leadership task much more manageable. This way of thinking about the leadership task, however, does add weight to the argument that leaders' success will typically depend on devoting their attention to a small number of priorities.

EMPIRICAL TEST OF THE FOUR PATHS THEORY OF ACTION

The original empirical test of the Four Paths theory of action (Leithwood, Patten, et al., 2010) used LSA online survey evidence from 1,445 teachers in 199 schools. The survey measured variables or conditions on each of the Four Paths, as well as the set of leadership practices described in Chapter 2. Grades 3 and 6 math and literacy achievement data were provided by the province's annual testing program (Ontario's Educational Quality and Accountability Program). The 2006 Canadian Census data provided a composite measure of school socioeconomic status used as a control variable.

Results of this initial study indicated that the Four Paths, as a whole, explained 43 percent of the variation in students' math and language achievement. Variables or conditions on the Rational, Emotional, and Family Paths explained similarly significant amounts of that variation, while variables on the Organizational Path were not as strongly related to student achievement. Leadership, as it was measured in this study, had its greatest influence on the Organizational Path and least influence on the Family Path.

LSA's theory of action has had a strong influence on the LSA Steering Team's decisions about future priorities. But it has also been taken up by districts and schools as a framework for guiding their improvement efforts. The next section of this chapter illustrates how one district made use of the theory of action. The story was written by those leading the literacy improvement efforts described in the story.

A Story About a District's Use of LSA's Theory of Action to Improve Student Literacy[3]

Over a two-year period, selected elementary and secondary teachers (Grades 8 and 9) were engaged in a most rewarding professional learning experience. Our cross-panel collaborative inquiry in literacy was influenced in its choice of priorities by the LSA theory of action: It focused on instruction, academic press, and collaborative inquiry (variables on the Rational Path); it developed trust, as well as a sense of collective efficacy, among teachers (variables on the Emotional Path); and it reshaped our organization of instructional time (a variable on the Organizational Path).

Inquiry assumes that "the answers are within," and this assumption was fundamental to our work. We began this work with a question about which we were curious: How can we merge the strengths found within both secondary and elementary panels to create a more consistent approach to teaching language arts and English with the goal of increasing student achievement? The starting point for our inquiry about how to answer this question was the belief that if collaborative relationships can be created between Grade 8 classroom

---

[3]This story was written by Dan Trainor, Jennifer DeCoff, and Eric Sabatini, Niagara Catholic District School Board. Reproduced with permission.

teachers and Grade 9 English teachers, then a more consistent and effective approach to teaching language arts and English will develop and student achievement in literacy will increase in the intermediate grades.

Teachers, in collaboration with our intermediate consultant, were able to construct their own inquiry based on professional reflection and observation. Initially, teachers from three of our secondary schools were linked to their associated elementary schools (five in total). Teachers and principals from these schools were invited to join the inquiry on instructional practice in Grades 8 and 9 literacy and be given a year in which to conduct their work. Teachers from both of these grades had the opportunity to observe each other's teaching and learning and engage in dialogue about what they observed and the instructional supports that were in place for that work. The expectation was that their observations would prompt them to create opportunities for coplanning and coteaching. These staff members wanted to see how "it all worked in each other's rooms." They wanted to challenge and/or confirm their own perceptions of the most productive Grade 8 and Grade 9 environments for learning.

We gained a greater understanding and appreciation of both panels and an affirmation of practices for successful transitions. (participating teacher in Year 1)

Teachers were then provided with release time to analyze provincial curriculum documents for language arts/English/literacy. Their analysis dispelled many myths about the curriculum, identified the "big ideas" in the curriculum, and clarified essential learnings for students in the intermediate years (Grades 7–10). This learning was crucial to the construction of inquiry lessons for our students. Teachers were able to appreciate the continuum of learning expected within the curriculum and from their observations; they were able to see the development of their students' skills related to the language arts/English/literacy curriculum. Our teachers easily and confidently spoke about what their students "know and can do" based on the curriculum expectations. From that knowledge, they were able to coplan lessons for the coteaching component of our inquiry.

The reflective learning from these many experiences was recorded in group dialogue sessions and individual research interviews. Students in all of the

(Continued)

classroom settings were interviewed about the coteaching and the transition from Grade 8 to Grade 9. Our understanding of this teaching and learning opportunity from the cross-panel inquiry is captured in the words of our researcher and our students:

> The co-teaching partners displayed a synergistic relationship which maintained the pace and flow of the lesson, keeping the students engaged. The teachers complimented each other and exemplified a competent and powerful instructional approach. (researcher)

> With two teachers, they could help out more and we got the point of the poem and a better understanding. (secondary student)

> Before this project, my answer would have been a level 2 answer, but after this project and learning the steps my answer will be closer to a level 4. (secondary student)

The cross-panel structure of our inquiry reduced communication barriers between our elementary and secondary schools and the instructional impact on students was believed to be substantial. Many of our secondary teachers were captivated by the "high-yield strategies" used in our elementary schools and were able to see how students could develop automaticity and self-regulation from these instructional strategies.

Teachers collaborated to construct common instructional practices for improving student learning and to improve transitions for students from Grade 8 to 9. Many of our secondary schools created dedicated Grade 9 literacy classrooms in response to what they had learned. The comment of one secondary principal captures the momentum and power of this inquiry in his school. He said,

> I believe my teachers understand what's happening in the elementary level and how elementary teachers are able to move their students forward in literacy. I can see our teachers starting to use many of the same strategies observed in the elementary panel, maybe not to the same degree, but they are seeing that we can incorporate some of these other practices. (secondary principal)

The power and momentum of this inquiry was extended and energized by the challenges we faced and the responses we developed:

- Teacher concerns—Open conversations were encouraged that allowed teachers to move from being familiar to establishing trust with each other leading to learning.

- Sustainability—To address the high turnover of ENG 1P classroom teachers, the secondary principal was committed, after a year, to make the ENG 1P position one of consistency and not a long-term occasional position.

- Secondary classroom environment—ENG classrooms were transient, which doesn't allow for a classroom rich in stimuli and limits the use of posted learning goals, success criteria, anchor charts, word walls, etc. The secondary principal decided to delegate specific classrooms to ENG 1P and 1A to foster consistency.

- Documentation of results—Results from the first year of our work created a demand from those involved to document the work in the second year. Participants wanted to learn more about the impact of the inquiry and how it was improving student achievement. So researchers from Brock University were hired to document the results.

Teacher skepticism about new initiatives is common and often justified. This project managed to address such questions as, "Why?" "What is this now about?" "How long is this going to last?" and "Is this the new flavor of the month?" The open-ended opportunity provided by our collaborative inquiry allowed everyone involved opportunities for self-directed learning. Each participant had a voice in helping to design his or her own learning; they all behaved as risk-takers and found success within their safe teaching/learning classrooms.

The project started with a focus on student transitions but turned into a profound multilevel learning experience for most of those involved; they had never been part of a professional learning experience that was so powerful and held such limitless possibilities. We have collected cross-panel participant teachers' feedback about their learning. To enrich our work, we have also recorded our students' reflections on the coteaching lessons. The research carried out on the cross-panel inquiry has also captured the influence of the principal as a colearner and leader in the process. The starting point for our project was the assumption that if teachers and principals engaged in collaborative inquiry about their planning and teaching for Grades 7–10, then they would see positive results in instructional practices and student achievement.

CONCLUSION

Several important implications for practice emerged from the results of the development and testing of LSA's theory of action. One implication for practicing leaders arose from identification of largely neglected bodies of knowledge and skills that should be part of leadership preparation and ongoing professional development. Among variables associated with each of the Four Paths, some have been a common focus of attention by school leaders and those providing leadership development experiences for many years (primarily those on the Rational and Organizational Paths). But many variables on both the Emotional and Family Paths have been largely neglected, even though results of the LSA study and many others suggest that such variables are likely to have at least comparable effects on student learning.

The results of the framework development and testing, secondly, also challenged the dominant narrative about ideal forms of school leadership, one saturated in the language of instruction. Evidence highlighted by the Four Paths suggests that even on the Rational Path, some school-level variables (e.g., academic emphasis and disciplinary climate) have impacts on student learning that easily rival the effects of those instructional variables that principal leaders are typically admonished to focus on but typically feel only moderately able to improve (e.g., specific instruction strategies, teachers' questioning techniques).[4] LSA, as a result, continues to advance forms of instruction (e.g., knowledge building, as described in Chapter 9) that hold considerable promise of making a difference but by no means restricts its attention to instructional improvement alone. The Four Paths theory of action now serves as a touchstone for the LSA Steering Team when making decisions about next steps in the project. The framework is also being used by project members to help guide their district and school improvement efforts, as the story included in this chapter illustrates.

---

[4]Adding additional weight to this implication about the range of variables, other than just instruction, on which leaders might focus their improvement efforts are the results of a recent meta-analytic review of evidence about the effects of interventions aimed at enhancing students' motivation to learn (Lazowski & Hulleman, 2016). Results from this review suggest substantially larger effects on student performance of efforts to improve their motivation to learn, as compared with comprehensive school reform programs, the majority of which are focused on classroom instruction (effect sizes of .52 and .11, respectively).

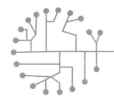

KNOWLEDGE BUILDING/KNOWLEDGE CREATION

Education for a Knowledge Society

At the time of this writing, leadership networks were one of LSA's two main priorities while knowledge building (KB)/ knowledge creation was the second. Knowledge building is the production and continual improvement of ideas of value to a community. Teachers engage students as members of a community, each needed and respected for the unique contributions they bring to the community. Students build on each other's ideas and bring ideas together in new ways, taking collective responsibility for creating more powerful ideas and artifacts out of the diversity of their ideas. Technology helps members to network with others within and beyond their local community; it also helps them use authoritative sources constructively to sustain idea improvement. Knowledge building is synonymous with knowledge creation. The term *knowledge building* was used because educators must enable building with ideas and the contexts that sustain it. Sustained creative work with ideas requires

---

[1]Professor Marlene Scardamalia made significant contributions to the development of this chapter.

community and environmental supports so that students are enculturated into contexts where idea improvement is the norm reflected in community knowledge.

Both priorities continued and extended LSA's sustained commitment to collaborative inquiry as a process for improving the authentic learning of educators and students alike. The priorities are mutually supportive. Leadership networks engaged their members in collaborative inquiry about improving conditions that, indirectly, enable student learning; KB engages teachers, students, and others in collaborative inquiry directly influencing such learning. This chapter helps to illustrate how this coherent orientation toward learning contributed to the sense making of all those involved. The focus is on implementation in LSA schools. For a more in-depth understanding about the nature of KB and evidence about its consequences for students, see research cited in this chapter.

This chapter also helps illustrate LSA's two approaches to leadership development outlined in Chapter 4, a provider, accelerator, and catalyst of professional development for school leaders, as well as part of a province-wide strategy for the implementation of innovations. As leaders and their networks became immersed in efforts to implement KB, they learned much more about the functioning of effective professional learning communities, the meaning of "deep understanding," and how they could facilitate the work of their teachers. After two years of experience helping staffs use KB in classrooms, principals developed much more sophisticated understandings of what it meant to be an instructional leader. LSA's work with KB paralleled efforts by the Ministry of Education, working directly with three school districts, to implement KB. Evidence from LSA's evaluations of early KB implementation was largely replicated by evaluations of KB work in the three ministry-sponsored districts.

THE MOTIVATION FOR ADOPTING KNOWLEDGE BUILDING

Collaborative inquiry has been viewed as a process for innovation, as well as for adapting, extending, and refining selected approaches to effective instruction found in broader research literatures. LSA's initial conception of effective instruction was based on a synthesis of evidence available in 2005–06 about effective instruction in both math and language in the elementary grades. Prompted by evidence from the first two annual evaluations of only modest impact, however, this initial conception evolved into support for "focused instruction," an approach to instruction across disciplines and grades identified in an important study by Wahlstrom and Louis (2008) and described (but not named) quite extensively in John Hattie's (2009) remarkable book titled *Visible Learning*. However, LSA's annual evaluations continued to find only weak contributions to student achievement of this approach to instruction.

During this same period, it should be noted, neither school districts nor the Ministry of Education itself were able to offer demonstrably more effective approaches to instruction, although they struggled mightily to do so. Declining scores on provincial math tests beginning about 2010, in spite of enormous efforts to stem the decline, are one indication of this struggle. As earlier chapters indicated, LSA's annual evaluations have demonstrated significant effects on achievement of most other key learning conditions included in LSA's theory of action but not for classroom instruction, whatever the approach measured at the time.

LSA remained committed to helping school leaders improve classroom instruction, however. In 2013, LSA began to explore an approach called "knowledge building" through the formation of a substantial partnership with its originators, Professors Scardamalia and Bereiter at Ontario Institute for Studies in Education, University of Toronto. Knowledge building is built on decades of research and theory in the learning sciences by Scardamalia and Bereiter, with substantial contributions to what was described in Chapter 5 as socioconstructivist perspectives on learning. The first of many research investigations showing the impact of knowledge building on student achievement and higher-order thinking was based on their work in an inner-city school in Toronto: students in knowledge-building classrooms showed increased scores on the Canadian Test of Basic Skills (language, reading, and vocabulary skills for both first-year and second-year knowledge-building students), with greater gains with more use, when compared with a control group (Scardamalia et al., 1992); research reported ever since, from Ontario and internationally (Chen & Hong, 2016), has shown consistently positive results in student achievement, including math problem solving, math talk, and writing, as well as significant advances that map onto global competencies and "twenty-first-century skills" (e.g., collaborative processes, inquiry processes, deep learning/scientificness, rotating leadership, epistemic complexity, and measures of vocabulary use that show students using concepts that exceed curriculum expectations).

LSA's motivation for adopting knowledge building also relates to the LSA theory of action, as shown in Figure 7.4. As indicated in Chapter 7, there are productive cross-overs and intersections between paths. This is further conveyed in the specific knowledge-building theory of action shown in Figure 8.1 indicating support for work along each of the four paths: rational, emotions, organizational, and family. Principal–teacher teams working within a LSA Knowledge Building Innovation Network pilot project demonstrate work along all four paths.

KNOWLEDGE BUILDING

Theoretical and empirical justification for Scardamalia and Bereiter's knowledge-building approach can be found in their many publications with students and colleagues (e.g., Chen, Scardamalia, & Bereiter, 2015; Ma, Matsuzawa, Chen, & Scardamalia, 2016; Resendes, Scardamalia, Bereiter, Chen, & Halewood, 2015; Scardamalia & Bereiter, 2006) while the stories included in the final two sections of this chapter provide "close to the ground" accounts of what KB can look like in practice. This section of the chapter touches briefly on central features of KB while the following section describes LSA's efforts to support knowledge building in the classrooms of members' schools. Much more information about using KB can be found in two new LSA publications (Resendes & Dobbie, 2017a, 2017b).

Selecting knowledge building as one of its central priorities accomplished several important objectives for LSA: it extended LSA's commitment to collaborative inquiry from staff to students, it addressed growing interest across the provincial school system in so-called twenty-first-century skills, and it offered a vision of classrooms as learning/knowledge-creating organizations. Scardamalia and

FIGURE 8.1 A Knowledge-Building Theory of Action for LSA

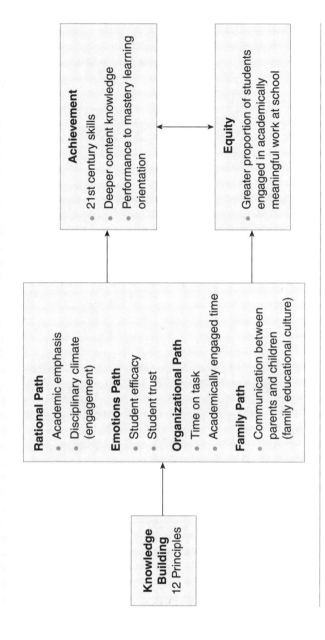

Knowledge Building
12 Principles

Rational Path
- Academic emphasis
- Disciplinary climate (engagement)

Emotions Path
- Student efficacy
- Student trust

Organizational Path
- Time on task
- Academically engaged time

Family Path
- Communication between parents and children (family educational culture)

Achievement
- 21st century skills
- Deeper content knowledge
- Performance to mastery learning orientation

Equity
- Greater proportion of students engaged in academically meaningful work at school

Source: Leithwood, 2015.

Bereiter's prior work had produced increasingly sophisticated ways of engaging students in constructing "deep understandings" about concepts and ideas found in most school curricula ("big ideas"). This work also led to the development and ongoing refinement of a computer program, now called Knowledge Forum, which assists students, acting as a community, to build knowledge together. As Scardamalia and Bereiter (2006) explain, "in Knowledge Building theory, pedagogy, and technology, students' work is primarily valued for what it contributes to the community and secondarily for what it reveals about individual students' knowledge" (p. 98). They stress that community and individual achievement are mutually reinforcing forces, however, and should not be seen in opposition to one another.

Community knowledge building is valued as a key goal for education because it mirrors the real world of knowledge creation, provides a place for everyone, and addresses expectations for those who will work in contexts where generating new knowledge is the job. Available evidence indicates that personal knowledge development (the conventional expectation of schools) occurs hand in hand with community knowledge building (e.g., Chen & Hong, 2016).

Knowledge building is principles driven rather than procedures driven. The twelve principles, captured in Figure 8.2, map directly on to fundamentals of real-world knowledge creation and socio-constructivist perspectives on the nature of learning and how it can be nurtured. In addition to summarizing the twelve principles, Figure 8.2 explains how Knowledge Forum technology assists students by engaging them directly in the high-level knowledge-creating processes that have resulted in advances in student achievement and global competencies.

FIGURE 8.2 Knowledge Building Principles Illustrated

REAL IDEAS, AUTHENTIC PROBLEMS

Socio-cognitive dynamics: Knowledge problems arise from efforts to understand the world. Ideas produced or appropriated are as real as things touched and felt. Problems are ones that learners really care about—usually very different from textbook problems and puzzles.

Technological dynamics: *Knowledge Forum* creates a culture for creative work with ideas. Notes and views serve as direct reflections of the core work of the organization and of the ideas of its creators.

IMPROVABLE IDEAS

Socio-cognitive dynamics: All ideas are treated as improvable. Participants work continuously to improve the quality, coherence, and utility of ideas. For such work to prosper, the culture must be one of psychological safety, so that people feel safe in taking risks—revealing ignorance, voicing half-baked notions, giving and receiving criticism.

Technological dynamics: *Knowledge Forum* supports recursion in all aspects of its design—there is always a higher level, there is always opportunity to revise. Background operations reflect change: continual improvement, revision, theory refinement.

IDEA DIVERSITY

Socio-cognitive dynamics: Idea diversity is essential to the development of knowledge advancement, just as biodiversity is essential to the success of an ecosystem. To understand an idea is to understand the ideas that surround it, including those that stand in contrast to it. Idea diversity creates a rich environment for ideas to evolve into new and more refined forms.

Technological dynamics: Bulletin boards, discussion forums, and so forth, provide opportunities for diversity of ideas but they only weakly support interaction of ideas. In *Knowledge Forum,* facilities for linking ideas and for bringing different combinations of ideas together in different notes and views promote the interaction that makes productive use of diversity.

RISE ABOVE

Socio-cognitive dynamics: Creative knowledge building entails working toward more inclusive principles and higher-level formulations of problems. It means learning to work with diversity, complexity and messiness, and out of that achieve new syntheses. By moving to higher planes of understanding knowledge builders transcend trivialities and oversimplifications and move beyond current best practices.

Technological dynamics: In expert knowledge building teams, as in *Knowledge Forum,* conditions to which people adapt change as a result of the successes of other people in the environment. Adapting means adapting to a progressive set of conditions that keep raising the bar. Rise-above notes and views support unlimited embedding of ideas in increasingly advanced structures, and support emergent rather than fixed goals.

EPISTEMIC AGENCY

Socio-cognitive dynamics: Participants set forth their ideas and negotiate a fit between personal ideas and ideas of others, using contrasts to spark and sustain knowledge advancement rather than depending on others to chart that course for them. They deal with problems of goals,

(Continued)

(Continued)

motivation, evaluation, and long-range planning that are normally left to teachers or managers.

Technological dynamics: *Knowledge Forum* provides support for theory construction and refinement and for viewing ideas in the context of related but different ideas. Scaffolds for high level knowledge processes are reflected in the use and variety of epistemological terms (such as conjecture, wonder, hypothesize, and so forth), and in the corresponding growth in conceptual content.

COMMUNITY KNOWLEDGE, COLLECTIVE RESPONSIBILITY

Socio-cognitive dynamics: Contributions to shared, top-level goals of the organization are prized and rewarded as much as individual achievements. Team members produce ideas of value to others and share responsibility for the overall advancement of knowledge in the community.

Technological dynamics: *Knowledge Forum's* open, collaborative workspace holds conceptual artifacts that are contributed by community members. Community membership is defined in terms of reading and building-on the notes of others, ensuring that views are informative and helpful for the community, linking views in ways that demonstrate view interrelationships. More generally, effectiveness of the community is gauged by the extent to which all participants share responsibility for the highest levels of the organization's knowledge work.

DEMOCRATIZING KNOWLEDGE

Socio-cognitive dynamics: All participants are legitimate contributors to the shared goals of the community; all take pride in knowledge advances achieved by the group. The diversity and divisional differences represented in any organization do not lead to separations along knowledge have/have-not or innovator/non-innovator lines. All are empowered to engage in knowledge innovation.

Technological dynamics: There is a way into the central knowledge space for all participants; analytic tools allow participants to assess evenness of contributions and other indicators of the extent to which all members do their part in a joint enterprise.

SYMMETRIC KNOWLEDGE ADVANCEMENT

Socio-cognitive dynamics: Expertise is distributed within and between communities. Symmetry in knowledge advancement results from knowledge exchange and from the fact that to give knowledge is to get knowledge.

Technological dynamics: *Knowledge Forum* supports virtual visits and the co- construction of views across teams, both within and between communities. Extended communities serve to embed ideas in increasingly broad social contexts. Symmetry in knowledge work is directly reflected in the flow and reworking of information across views and databases of different teams and communities.

PERVASIVE KNOWLEDGE BUILDING

Socio-cognitive dynamics: Knowledge building is not confined to particular occasions or subjects but pervades mental life—in and out of school.

Technological dynamics: *Knowledge Forum* encourages knowledge building as the central and guiding force of the community's mission, not as an add-on. Contributions to collective resources reflect all aspects of knowledge work.

CONSTRUCTIVE USES OF AUTHORITATIVE SOURCES

Socio-cognitive dynamics: To know a discipline is to be in touch with the present state and growing edge of knowledge in the field. This requires respect and understanding of authoritative sources, combined with a critical stance toward them.

Technological dynamics: *Knowledge Forum* encourages participants to use authoritative sources, along with other information sources, as data for their own knowledge building and idea-improving processes. Participants are encouraged to contribute new information to central resources, to reference and build-on authoritative sources; bibliographies are generated automatically from referenced resources.

KNOWLEDGE BUILDING DISCOURSE

Socio-cognitive dynamics: The discourse of knowledge building communities results in more than the sharing of knowledge; the knowledge itself is refined and transformed through the discursive practices of the community—practices that have the advancement of knowledge as their explicit goal.

Technological dynamics: *Knowledge Forum* supports rich intertextual and inter- team notes and views and emergent rather than predetermined goals and workspaces. Revision, reference, and annotation further encourage participants to identify shared problems and gaps in understanding and to advance understanding beyond the level of the most knowledgeable individual.

EMBEDDED AND TRANSFORMATIVE ASSESSMENT

Socio-cognitive dynamics: Assessment is part of the effort to advance knowledge—it is used to identify problems as the work proceeds and is

(Continued)

embedded in the day-to-day workings of the organization. The community engages in its own internal assessment, which is both more fine-tuned and rigorous than external assessment, and serves to ensure that the community's work will exceed the expectations of external assessors.

Source: Scardamalia, M. (2001). Socio-Cognitive and Technological Determinants of Knowledge Building, http://lcp.cite.hku.hk/resources/KBSN/Q1/KB_Principle.html

CREATING INTEREST IN KNOWLEDGE BUILDING AND THE CAPACITY FOR IMPLEMENTATION

Knowledge building was first introduced to LSA members at the 2013 fall symposium. Scardamalia and Bereiter's presentation during that symposium stressed knowledge building as a way of life for many adults working in knowledge-creating organizations. Knowledge building in schools connects students to that world, encourages students to take more responsibility for their own learning, and pushes students to deeper levels of understanding about the big ideas in all of the disciplines they study.

Knowledge building, explained Scardamalia, can be contrasted to approaches in which the teacher teaches the curriculum and develops the tasks for students to undertake; the students complete the designated tasks. Under these conditions, school is about students doing well on assigned tasks, even though they may not understand them and have no power or control with regard to them. Rather than tasks and activities being the central focus, in KB, students' ideas are central—to be built on and improved by the community. As in knowledge-creating organizations, there are tasks, but they are embedded in broader goals that give meaning to them. In schools, in contrast, the task is frequently an end it its own right, and students are blind to curriculum expectations set out by experts that represent the broader goals. In knowledge building, teachers are encouraged to transfer epistemic agency to students— engage them at the very highest levels of goal setting and monitoring achievements, including engaging students in discussions of curriculum standards. Teachers are aware of curriculum goals, why not students? Accordingly, as reflected in the "Story About Knowledge Building in Science Classrooms," knowledge-building teachers will frequently engage students in discussion of curriculum goals related to challenges students set for themselves. The goals they set for themselves are often goals of understanding (e.g., to understand body systems, what makes for a healthy nation, what creates inflation). Pursuing these in the context of broader goals and expectations positions students to responsibly monitor progress: Is their questioning and research getting anywhere? Are there relevant concepts they have not yet explored? Do their ideas come together in a coherent whole, or do they just have disconnected ideas? Are they exceeding curriculum expectations? As they proceed, teams of students continue to formulate key questions surrounding areas of interest and relevance, gather information, develop ideas and theories, refine them in light of new information, and so forth.

Community knowledge and collective responsibility are core components of a knowledge-building community. Knowledge is shared by everyone, and everyone shares responsibility for the overall advancement of community knowledge. Often, the information uncovered as they search authoritative sources is at an advanced level, requiring students to work hard to develop their understanding of the material. They regularly share the questions they pose and information they gather, as well as discuss it and develop theories based on it. This ongoing process results in continual improvement. An important KB principle, explained Bereiter during the symposium, is pervasive knowledge building; success is achieved when all succeed. This encompasses the belief that everyone should be helped and that everyone should be part of the movement forward. When a team succeeds, each individual has a sense of succeeding.

The provincial symposium, during which Scardamalia and Bereiter explained the rationale and theory underlying KB, was followed by a series of regional workshops for all LSA members and their staffs interested in beginning to use knowledge-building approaches in their schools. As the workshops got underway, LSA revised a part of its annual evaluation in order to track progress with members' efforts to use KB in their schools and classrooms. Results from the evaluation during the first two years of KB use are summarized in the next two sections.

THE FIRST YEAR OF
KNOWLEDGE-BUILDING IMPLEMENTATION

By mid-winter of 2014, best estimates suggested about fifty schools and 150 classrooms were in the early stages of implementing knowledge building. The annual evaluation that year conducted phone interviews with a sample of about three dozen principals, teachers, and district leaders about their experiences. Overall, these interviews indicated that knowledge building was being used in many areas of the curriculum. Among the many types of assistance provided by LSA for implementing knowledge building, those providing direct guidance about how to introduce knowledge building into the classroom were viewed as most helpful.

Knowledge building required significant changes in the instructional practices of most teachers, changes requiring teachers to become partners in learning with their students, to change from being the holders of all knowledge to encouraging students to engage in asking questions and building on each other's knowledge and experience (collective responsibility for community knowledge).

The greatest challenge for teachers in the early stages of implementing knowledge building in their classrooms was letting go of control over key aspects of instruction and trusting meaningful learning would occur as students share responsibility and become effective agents in advancing community knowledge (epistemic agency). It was proving very difficult for teachers to adopt the role of facilitators for students as their students exercised greater initiative in identifying what to learn and how to learn it (real ideas and authentic problems). Advancing the frontiers of students' knowledge entailed finding out what students already knew, helping students identify what they needed to understand, and then building on that knowledge, helping students set the direction for their own learning.

Principals and district leaders reported using a large handful of strategies for assisting teachers and principals as they pushed forward with their knowledge-building efforts. Providing additional time and professional development were considered useful to both groups, as were efforts by principals to colearn with their teacher colleagues. The majority of principals, teachers, and district leaders believed that progress was being made by teachers in their implementation of knowledge building and by students in their motivation to learn, their engagement in the classroom, and the depth and complexity of the ideas they were developing.

As this summary begins to suggest, the interviews reflected attention by principals, teachers, and system leaders to four of the knowledge-building principles outlined in Figure 8.1. The interviews also provided some evidence of a weak form of collective responsibility for community knowledge.

While the interviewees did not indicate just how authentically these five principles were reflected in work with students, these principles were at least top of mind in the case of many LSA participants. The five KB principles reflect ideas and practices that had been part of the LSA project for the previous half-dozen years prior to introducing KB, one way or another. So it is easy to imagine a preoccupation with these principles, to begin with, on the part of school staffs; it is how they are beginning to make sense of this initiative—by relating it to ideas and practices with which they are already familiar.

Very little of what was said by interviewees, however, touched on detailed components of the principles that map onto fundamentals of knowledge creation or the remaining seven knowledge-building principles.

The challenge going forward, concluded the evaluation, was to help school staffs come to grips with deeper issues regarding all principles and how these seven more novel knowledge-building principles and related practices could be incorporated into their approaches to instruction.

The evaluation also made three additional recommendations to the Steering Team and LSA school leaders:

1. *Persistently communicate the integrity of the research and theory underlying LSA's approach to knowledge building.* LSA's decision to advocate for an approach to knowledge building based on the work of Scardamalia and Bereiter was especially important because it is the most sophisticated and mature work available. As implementation proceeds, other less well-developed and less demanding

alternatives may well appear attractive to some project participants. This recommendation, then, is to do whatever is reasonable
to prevent erosion of the chosen approach—for example, argue for
innovative advances relative to the twelve knowledge-building principles and related practices; as much as possible, adopt the technological support available for the approach; and, perhaps especially,
facilitate the development of a deep understanding of the theory
and related evidence underlying this approach to knowledge building. Such an understanding will go some distance toward building
implementers' flexibility in effectively using this approach to knowledge building in the many different contexts of their work.

2. *Guard against cooptation.* Even for many staff members enthusiastic about implementing knowledge-building approaches to
some of their instruction, inadvertent cooptation of the approach
will be a constant danger. As the interviews found, at least four of
the KB principles suggest practices that resemble practices with
which many teachers are very familiar, in part because of previous
LSA efforts. The danger is that they will not continue to improve
their practices, assuming a "been there, done that" stance, and fail
to incorporate the additional and more novel components and
principles that are key to realizing the goals of knowledge building, the result being not much additional value added for students.
So this recommendation was to help school staffs come to grips
with the novel components of knowledge-building principles and
show how these principles map on to the real world of knowledge
creation and how knowledge-building practices can be incorporated into their approaches to instruction.

3. *Keep knowledge building in perspective.* Knowledge building is
particularly well designed to help students achieve complex objectives considered increasingly important in Ontario and much of the
rest of the developed world. These are objectives concerned with
critical thinking, self-regulation, the ability to contribute productively to knowledge creation, "twenty-first-century learning," and
global competencies. That said, it will be difficult to realize the targeted value of the knowledge building without a sense of rejection
of other forms of effective instruction aimed at more conventional
objectives. But in the real world of knowledge creation, groups
and individuals make use of lectures, practice, direct instruction,
and other instructional media and forms of engagement. So this
recommendation was to help some staff members avoid "throwing

out the baby with the bathwater." Gains in staff capacities resulting from years of effort aimed at improving the teaching of reading, for example, need to be protected. The goal is to have the excitement of building knowledge help drive an interest in reading; gains in reading and vocabulary with knowledge building complement basic skills by having others read and build on one's ideas.

THE SECOND YEAR OF
KNOWLEDGE-BUILDING IMPLEMENTATION

LSA continued to provide substantial support to members implementing knowledge building throughout the second year of use. (About seventy-five schools and two hundred classrooms were involved at this point.) This support included regional workshops, networking with advanced users of knowledge building, and the hiring of an LSA staff member with special expertise in knowledge building (Monica Resendes, a former doctoral student of Professor Scardamalia).

Building on the interview evidence about knowledge-building implementation collected during the first year, the following year's evaluation was based on survey data from fifty-three respondents who claimed to be engaged with knowledge building in their classroom. It is important to note that there was no check on actual use. As indicated previously, participants mention principles that correspond with familiar practices, with no indication of distinctive knowledge-building practices, so reports could reflect former familiar practices only. Significant advances in student achievement and global competences, including results from the original knowledge-building school in Ontario (Scardamalia et al., 1992), are based on actual engagement in knowledge building. As elaborated later, survey data can be misleading, although respondents' perceptions are always important. The most important results and recommendations from this study are summarized here:

1. *Student outcomes:* The survey asked a general question about the extent to which implementing KB has contributed to significantly improved learning on the part of many students who have struggled with more typical approaches to instruction. Responses to this question signified a perception of very little such improvement. Ratings of improvement on a series of more specific outcomes

indicated a judgment of "very little" to "some" improvement. Among the subject-related skills, problem solving was rated highest. Depth and complexity of idea development is rated highest of the general cognitive capacities. And "willingness to collaborate with peers in order to advance learning" was rated highest among four measured dispositions.

Evidence about student outcomes is rightly and inevitably of particular interest to those considering the implementation of KB in their classrooms and schools or encouraging such implementation across their districts. It is important to appreciate, accordingly, that these results do not address what can be accomplished through actual and significant use of KB practices but rather serve as a baseline for judging starting points of familiarity with knowledge-building concepts.

As the survey indicated, most of those who responded were in the very early stages of implementing KB in their schools and classrooms, and most secondary school respondents did not yet know what areas of the curriculum had been chosen for KB implementation. The evaluation recommended that the same set of questions about student outcomes be readministered about the same time next year. LSA is also beginning to produce data regarding actual use, and this should be given greater weight, as it is through measures of actual engagement in knowledge building that significant advances in student achievement and higher-order competencies have been found.

2. *Knowledge-building principles:* Results suggested that some KB principles, at least nominally, were sufficiently familiar to staffs and sufficiently part of their existing repertoires as to become a part of their KB implementation initiatives. This seemed to be the case, for example, with "democratizing knowledge" and using "real ideas and authentic problems." However, principles such as "democratizing knowledge" are often used to signify engaging everyone at some level, but knowledge building requires actual building on ideas and evidence of knowledge advances on the part of all. Principles such as "rise above," requiring ideas not just be built on but brought together in more integrated and powerful ways, and "symmetric knowledge advancement," in which advances beyond those of the local community are mirrored in the knowledge searches and uses of the community, represent

demanding knowledge work that must be engaged in reliably to produce knowledge advances. The evaluation recommended that future efforts to assist classroom implementation of KB would do well to emphasize how these principles can be used across the curriculum areas chosen for KB implementation.

3. *Challenges for students:* A large proportion of students were perceived to be experiencing all seven challenges identified in the survey. However, all students were believed to have difficulty in making the transition from class discussion to the use of Knowledge Forum and to have difficulty in formulating questions. The evaluation concluded that providing staffs with additional advice about how to assist students to address both of these challenges, in particular, seems warranted.

4. *Challenges for staff:* Results suggested that the majority of staff, like students, had been experiencing all of the challenges listed in the survey. But future assistance with two challenges, in particular, seemed in order. These challenges were "adapting to the forms of assessment called for when implementing knowledge building" and "figuring out how to help parents understand this approach to instruction for their student."

5. *Future supports:* Combining survey results about the value of past supports and the desirability of future supports points to the importance, going forward, of continuing to do the following:

- Provide release time for teachers
- Create opportunities for teachers to collaborate with one another and to visit other schools implementing KB practices with the aim of demonstrating practical ways of implementing KB in classrooms
- Help staffs develop assessment/evaluation practices in KB classrooms. Recent work shows that analytic tools built into Knowledge Forum are helping teachers engage students more productively. For example, the tools support the principle *embedded and transformative assessment* as teachers can quickly see actual patterns of student engagement. In response, they have developed impressive new practices to engage all students more productively and increased their capacity to democratize knowledge.

While the two rounds of evaluation point to important advances, as well as challenges for early KB users, they reveal little about the nature of KB use in classrooms—what a KB classroom looks and feels like. The next section of the chapter, written by the KB users themselves, help fill that gap and point to new forms of assessment/evaluation practices that help drive knowledge building forward.

A Story About Knowledge Building in Science Classrooms[2]

You might ask yourself, "What is knowledge building/knowledge creation? What does it look like, and how did our school begin to move in this direction? "Knowledge building" is the LSA Project's most recent initiative. It is a theoretically rich and highly developed approach to instruction aimed at developing students' deep understanding of big ideas and complex concepts. The technology Knowledge Forum is used to support the knowledge-building environment.

Our LSA School Team was first introduced to the knowledge-building concept when we attended the LSA Symposium in the fall of 2013. At the symposium, Jason Frenza (a grade 5 teacher) and I (principal) had the privilege of learning about the Twelve Principles of Knowledge Building that grew out of a history of research with the Laboratory School at the University of Toronto and the work of Professors Scardamalia and Bereiter.

Our discussions after attending the symposium left us with a lot of reservations about KB. We were not convinced that we would be able to achieve all of the expectations outlined in the curriculum and have enough evidence to support the assessment and evaluation of student work. We were rather skeptical about the whole idea.

Nevertheless, after the symposium, we participated in an LSA virtual session on knowledge building, and we gained a better understanding of what KB looks like and how we could implement it. After that session, Mr. Frenza and I sat at the table in my office, and I asked, "What do you think? Are you willing to try this?" He agreed to take a leap of faith and introduce knowledge building in his next science unit ("Structures and Mechanisms") that he was planning to start in January.

---

[2]This story was written by K. Dobbie and J. Frenza. Reproduced with permission.

This is where our story gets really interesting. Not only did Mr. Frenza introduce knowledge building and Knowledge Forum to his class, but he also spread his work to his teaching partners. They too are engaged now in knowledge building with their students, and we are learning together! Knowledge building has allowed our students to have a voice in their own learning while developing the skill set of a twenty-first-century learner. This process has opened up our students' thinking, and we have seen their ideas rise and their confidence increase.

Knowledge building is a unique form of inquiry-based learning, an approach to teaching and learning that places students' ideas and observations at the center of the learning experience. Educators play an active role throughout the process by establishing a culture in which ideas are respectfully challenged, tested, redefined, and viewed as improvable and move students from a position of wondering to a position of enacted understanding and further questioning (Scardamalia, 2002). Underlying this approach is the idea that both educators and students share responsibility for learning.

The remainder of this story describes what KB looked like in a Grade 5 class at St. Anthony of Padua in HCDSB; it is Mr. Frenza's response, in his own words, to the question, *How has knowledge building changed your approach to teaching and learning science in your Grade 5 classroom?*

How KB Processes Unfolded With My Students

My first step was to engage my students in the learning process by introducing them to the science curriculum document. This was a new approach for me and for my students. Together, we explored the big ideas and curriculum expectations in our next unit of study in science. We then proceeded to cocreate the learning goals together. My students then began to explore their natural curiosity by creating questions that they had related to the big ideas. Epistemic agency was at work in my classroom.

I had to take a step back and allow my students to explore and direct their own learning through student voice. As a teacher who has normally directed the learning process and meticulously planned out a unit with the end in mind, this new approach often had me doubting the value of the learning that would take place. I had lots of reservations; I was not convinced that we would be able to achieve all of the expectations outlined in the curriculum

(Continued)

(Continued)

and have enough evidence to support the assessment and evaluation of student work.

Nevertheless, my students and I together explored and decided on the learning activities that would take place. Out of our student inquiry came four critical activities that made student learning visible. These activities were as follows:

1. Knowledge-building circles

2. Knowledge-building reflections

3. Picture learning logs

4. My investigations

For each of these four activities, I cocreated, with my students, the success criteria that guided and supported their learning and allowed my students to successfully achieve the learning goals that we set together at the beginning of this journey.

1. *Knowledge-building circles* have proven to be a very powerful tool in allowing my students to share the knowledge they gained through the inquiry process. The knowledge-building circle allows them to share their knowledge and build upon the knowledge of others in the classroom. Putting into practice one of the twelve principles of knowledge building (knowledge-building discourse) has allowed me to witness firsthand the power and value of students learning from one another.

   Knowledge-building discourse is a central part of the inquiry process, one that provides teachers with rich opportunities to observe how students use what they know to solve problems of understanding. In particular, knowledge-building circles not only reveal the skills and content knowledge that students accumulate but also the manner in which they think about, interact with, and communicate their ideas.

   This process supports differentiated instruction, as it allows our students who sometimes struggle with the traditional pencil-and-paper tasks to communicate their learning and develop confidence in sharing their knowledge with their peers and teacher.

2. *Knowledge-building reflections* come after a knowledge-building circle has taken place. This provides students an opportunity to reflect on their

own learning and the learnings of others. Students share what they have learned from their student inquiry and build on their own theories and the theories that their classmates shared during the knowledge-building circles. Students question theories and create new questions about which they are still curious in relation to their learning goals.

I witnessed the development of higher-level questioning skills in my students. Instead of asking those simple knowledge and comprehension questions, students challenged themselves and others to ask rich and meaningful questions related to the real world.

3. *Picture learning logs* allow students to illustrate science concepts and theories in the form of a picture or diagram. This learning activity allows students to illustrate rich connections between science theories and concepts and their everyday lives.

4. *My investigations* involve hands-on science experiments. Students are given an opportunity to engage in science experiments that test their theories and answer their questions about science concepts and their learning goals. Once students complete their investigations, their follow-up activity is to complete a learning log whereby they reflect on the learning in the form of a lab report.

Using Knowledge Forum

Knowledge Forum (KF) supports knowledge-building discourse. It is an online community space where all ideas can live, grow, and develop organically. Building on the knowledge of others can begin small and take on a world of its own in a very small amount of time. Once the power of knowledge takes hold by using the scaffolds in KF to illustrate their theories and their learning, we witnessed firsthand how our students were engaged and excited about learning from each other. The students then take the scaffolds that they use in Knowledge Forum and use them in their conversations in the knowledge-building circles. Students can be heard saying, "My theory is . . . , I am going to add on . . . and I still wonder about . . ."

Through the use of Knowledge Forum, it became clear that all knowledge was valued within our community of learners. The more the students used KF, the more confident they became in sharing their knowledge with others. We witnessed how some knowledge went viral within minutes of it being posted on

(Continued)

(Continued)

the forum. Knowledge Forum is a valuable tool that allows teachers to differentiate instruction to meet the needs of all students, especially those who struggle with the traditional paper-and-pencil tasks.

The learning that is taking place through knowledge building is very powerful, very real, and very meaningful for our students. Our students are making rich connections to their everyday lives and the real world. Knowledge building has allowed our students to develop the skill set of a twenty-first-century learner. Our challenge now is to spread this good work so that we can become a knowledge-building school that enables all of our students to develop their potential.

Our greatest fear was not having enough evidence of student work to support assessment and evaluation. However, as knowledge building evolved in the classroom, it became very clear that there were multiple ways to assess and evaluate student learning.

Miniconferences take place while students are engaged in investigating a question. The teacher develops an understanding of student knowledge related to the learning goals. The rich discussions between teacher and students allowed students to go more deeply into their learning and illustrate meaningful connections.

Knowledge-building circles provide an opportunity for the teacher to assess expressive language and communication. They allow students to interact with each other by sharing diverse ideas and perspectives. Every child feels that his or her knowledge and contribution to the knowledge-building circle are valued and respected. All ideas are potentially good ideas, and we can build and learn from one another. I witnessed firsthand how my students build on each other's thinking. They really understand the knowledge-building principle of "improvable ideas." The role of the teacher is to guide the sharing of knowledge and support the students in relating their knowledge back to learning goals that they cocreated at the beginning of the unit. The teacher encourages students to ask higher-level thinking questions that challenge their theories and the theories of others.

Two Key Challenges

Knowledge building did not evolve without its challenges, two of which were especially demanding. The first and likely the greatest challenge for teachers was to relinquish complete control of student learning and share that control with students. This is not an easy task for a teacher who is used to directing and controlling the learning taking place in his or her classroom. However, once you let go, you quickly see the value in facilitating student learning and the motivation and engagement of your students will encourage you to continue this process. Teacher efficacy definitely increased as student learning became visible in the classroom. The fears that arose originally quickly began to dissipate as students immersed themselves in learning and wanted to continue the new way of learning.

A second key challenge was finding time. The time factor is always a challenge in any classroom. There never seems to be enough hours in the day. Giving yourself permission to be flexible on the journey with your students is a very valuable and rewarding experience. Often, what you intend to accomplish in one period can take two or three periods. However, the learning that has takes place is so powerful that you realize that the extra time spent on the learning was well worth it. You may have had to juggle your schedule and rob time from another subject, but in the end, it is worth it, and often, cross-curricular learning has taken place!!

Learning how to teach students to use the Knowledge Forum platform did not come without its challenges. However, in the end, students became the teachers to each other in learning to use this forum effectively. If you give students the tools, they can usually master problems much more quickly than we do as adults simply because we are sometimes less flexible in our thinking. Throughout this process, teaching and encouraging students to ask higher-level thinking questions was always a focus and a challenge. However, it was rewarding to witness students asking rich and meaningful questions.

Reflections on Our Success

Our success so far is huge. Through the implementation of KB, students, who in the past were completely disengaged in the learning process, were now taking charge of their own learning. Differentiated instruction allowed these students to demonstrate their knowledge in a variety of ways and feel confident about their learning. Students became the drivers of their own learning, and student voice was honored. Teachers became partners with their students in the learning process. Students' passion and excitement for learning flourished as they became more comfortable and confident as a community of knowledge builders.

(Continued)

(Continued)

When Ken Leithwood refers to the family path, part of LSA's theory of action, he speaks about the social and intellectual capital that students develop within their homes and how students bring that capital to school and share that knowledge with their peers. Engaging the home in the learning process is a "high leverage" option, as defined by Ken Leithwood.

Our use of the Knowledge Forum platform enabled our parents to become much more engaged in their child's learning; it became very clear to our parents how their children were embracing this new way of learning and thinking. Here is one parent's reflection on her child's learning journey through this process.

My son had the wonderful opportunity of participating in a knowledge building forum for several months in Mr Frenza's grade 5 class. This was a pilot project that his class and teacher participated in and the experience for him was very rewarding. While participating in knowledge building we found that our son was excited to bring homework home as he was involved in researching information that he found interesting. He was very enthusiastic and informed himself with the appropriate amount of info required but also went further to explore what else he could find on the topic. We found that knowledge building kept him engaged in what he was learning both at school and at home.

Knowledge building allowed him to retain the information that, he found easier as he was researching to inform himself and others and researching information that was interesting to him. When working in groups, he learned to interact well with others, learned from others and learned to respect others thoughts and opinions.

Another great benefit that our son gained from Knowledge building was how to use technology to benefit his education. He learned how to research, participate in online forums and post relevant information for himself and classmates to learn about.

Overall, we believe that knowledge building is a very valuable asset in the learning curriculum as it helped him feel more confident in his studies, engaged him when learning new topics and also prepared him for real life situations.

Why would we ever look back? Our successes have definitely outweighed our challenges. The dividends from our successes continue to grow and inspire us to spread this good work.

Our present Grade 6 students are knowledge-building ambassadors who have thrived and embraced this new way or thinking and learning. This work has impacted our pedagogy and thoughtful planning. Teachers are now activators rather than directors in the learning process. Giving students the opportunity to unlock their knowledge and share it with their peers allows students to become the drivers of their own learning.

By working collaboratively, teachers learn new and innovative practices that are relevant, current, and engaging to twenty-first-century learning in helping their students solve real-life, authentic problems. We have created a culture whereby students are comfortable in taking risks in their learning and are not afraid to go deeper with their thinking. As we introduce emerging strategies and techniques such as the Knowledge Forum, we are promoting twenty-first-century teaching and learning.

Our challenge now is to spread this good work so that we can become a knowledge-building school that enables all of our students to develop their potential. Our biggest payoff on this journey of knowledge building was the students' love of learning. Student success is at the heart of everything we do.

CONCLUSION

The stories that have been written for LSA about participants' uses of knowledge building in their classrooms and webinars in which teachers report advances mirror the same level of enthusiasm and estimates of student success reflected in this chapter's story. While relatively informal sources of evidence, the growing number of stories is consistent with the more systematic results of research on KB by Scardamalia and Bereiter and colleagues. So LSA's commitment to KB as a promising approach going forward seems justified for now.

One of the lessons learned by the project's Steering Committee through its long experience, however, is that initially very promising approaches often fall short in the long run: they are difficult to implement well, or they demand structures and supports that schools eventually seem unable to provide or sustain, or only early (enthusiastic) adopters seem able to get the promised results, and so forth. The evidence of value from "somewhere else" just can't be replicated by local evidence—on a large scale. It is this "large scale" criterion that seems especially difficult to meet—indeed, yet to be met by any educational approach. So while KB has yet to meet it, results from many nations with great cultural variation suggest education can indeed be brought into the real world of knowledge creation. In Ontario, work by over ten school boards across all curriculum areas is producing innovations by principals and teachers working together to open new possibilities in education.

Providing evidence about the value of KB on a large scale will be complicated by the ambitious nature of the student outcomes it claims to develop—deep knowledge about big ideas on the part of not just individual students but collaborating groups of students, along with residual capacities and dispositions for productive inquiry processes in the future. Oh! And improved math and language scores on provincial tests, as well. Embarking on the kind of systematic work required to provide this evidence promises to be the most significant challenge yet faced by LSA leaders. Of course, bringing education into the real world of knowledge creation represents a new challenge for education as a whole—a challenge requiring new means of assessment. Knowledge building is bringing new research tools to bear, as suggested in the prior story and further elaborated in recent accounts by teachers in the Knowledge Building Innovation Network webinars hosted by LSA. It is in keeping with LSA to take on major challenges and to engage in progressive refinement. The field of education itself is on a knowledge-building journey, and there is no expectation that the course will be easy.

Chapter 9

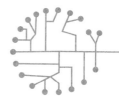

CREATING USEFUL KNOWLEDGE ABOUT LEADERSHIP NETWORKS

Taking It to the Next Level

LSA's multiple annual evaluations indicated that principal learning teams (PLTs) were consistently perceived to be of considerable value by most project members. Furthermore, among eleven different sources of professional learning, principals ranked PLTs second only to their own personal professional reading. Such consistent evidence of PLTs' value helped to ensure twelve years of continuing support for PLTs by the project Steering Team. Leaders were provided with many opportunities to learn from one another—to learn from those working in similar contexts and facing similar challenges. PLTs provided structures within which valuable procedural knowledge could be shared, critically reflected upon, and adapted for use in individual schools with the assistance of one's experienced peers.

In 2015, the Steering Team decided to undertake research aimed at providing evidence-informed guidelines about how existing PLTs could become even more valuable sources of school leaders' learning. This research, conducted on behalf of LSA by the project evaluator, is summarized in the next three sections of this chapter. The first section outlines some fundamental theoretical assumptions on which this research was based, while the second section summarizes the results of the two empirical studies completed by LSA to this point. A story about the work of one leadership network illustrates what some of the key research results look and feel like "on the ground" in the third and final section of the chapter.

FUNDAMENTAL ASSUMPTIONS ABOUT LEARNING IN NETWORKS

Leadership networks, such as LSA's principal learning teams, typically aim to build both the capacities of individual members and the school or district organization as a whole. A network, it is assumed, contributes to the capacity of individual members by exposing them to the practices, dispositions, and ideas of others faced with similar tasks and responsibilities; this is the knowledge diffusion goal of networks, one that exploits knowledge already developed by ensuring that such knowledge goes to scale. This will often be a crucial network goal because legitimate organizational concerns for efficiency and cost-effectiveness demand that the often-considerable price tag on original knowledge development be amortized over as many relevant people and contexts in the organization as possible.

A network is also a structure that, under the right conditions, is capable of stimulating potentially rich interactions among members, resulting in new and creative ideas or practices not initially part of the repertoire of any individual network member. The whole becomes more than the sum of its parts; this is the knowledge-creation goal of networks. Knowledge creation depends on meeting at least three closely related conditions. The first of the conditions required for knowledge creation is a willingness, on the part of participants, to collaborate together in the solving of some shared problem or the meeting of a shared purpose. While principals, for example, may regularly collaborate with their own staffs, many are still less familiar with the experience of collaborating with other principals in their district. In some districts a lack of trust and norms of competitiveness (perhaps nurtured by accountability policies) may give rise to resistance toward such collaboration.

A second condition for knowledge creation in collaborative contexts is a willingness, during collaborative interactions, to genuinely listen to the ideas of one's network colleagues. Such listening entails a conscious change in mindset, from one that is primarily about assimilation to one that is focused on adaptation. Assimilation is the default cognitive mechanism for people when striving to make sense of at least superficially new information. Assimilation seems to reduce the complexity involved in such sense making ("this so-called 'new' idea is simply a version of something I already know about, just described using different words"), but it produces almost no new learning. Adaptation, on the other hand, means that while you may see many similarities in the new information or idea that conform to your existing understandings, you also identify features of the new idea requiring some extension or reorganization of your understanding to fully grasp. Such extension and reorganization of your understanding *is* learning. And such learning is a personally creative act. Indeed, the conscious adoption of an adaptation mindset is a hallmark of expertise.

Knowledge creation in collaborative contexts also depends on the emergence of solutions or ideas that are not simply personally creative (individual learning) but are creative or novel and useful to the collaborating groups as a whole. To claim that "the whole is more than the sum of its parts" means that if network members interact together in productive ways, they will identify solutions or ideas that none of them individually would be likely to identify. Everyone has had personal experiences that conform to this assumption at some point in their lives, and there is considerable empirical evidence endorsing the possibility. But interactive processes resulting in objectively novel solutions or ideas are far too rare—and the processes far too inefficient—to use as the sole or even the normal form of solution or idea generation. So productive organizational learning in networks almost always infuses relevant ideas located in sources outside the network. Infusion of these relevant ideas is an especially key condition for progress when the goal of the network is exploration as distinct from exploitation.

Building on these ideas about how productive network interactions are able to exploit existing knowledge and mine the minds of their members and others, it is helpful to clarify the types of knowledge that network structures seem most likely to develop. Building on distinctions between propositional and procedural knowledge, as well as tacit and explicit knowledge, networks are particularly well suited to shining a light on the otherwise tacit procedural knowledge of their members.

Propositional knowledge is about ideas and concepts (addressing questions about what to do) while procedural knowledge is about steps to take, routines to follow, and processes for implementing some "what." Of course, these two types of knowledge are not independent of one another. You should not assume without further exploration, for example, that the procedures used for improving the literacy achievement in your school will also be effective for improving math achievement in your school, without at least considerable adaptation.

Tacit knowledge is what people carry around in their heads to guide their practice. Some of this knowledge is explicit—that is, it has or can be codified in some fashion. But much of it is not, and the difficulty of codifying tacit knowledge in conventional ways is a function of its level of detail and its contextual sensitivity. For example, an experienced principal who is quite expert at what she does carries around in her head a huge amount of detailed information about how best to respond to the wide array of "if–then" scenarios she has already and will likely again encounter in her school. While many of the "ifs" in these scenarios will have similarities to the "ifs" faced by other principals, some will be unique to her school, and almost all of the "thens" will be even more unique because of the particular circumstances and features of her students, staff, parent community, school organization, and own personal capacities and personal leadership resources.

Like her other expert principal colleagues, the practices of this principal are guided by tacit knowledge that she will have considerable difficulty making them explicit for herself, let alone others who might learn from them. Experts run on automatic pilot much of the time, taking over the cognitive controls only when they notice something unique that might require a custom-made response. So even personal reflection on one's own practices is severely limited by access to one's own tacit knowledge, and what one is able to make explicit may be only a rough approximation to one's tacit knowledge. The proportion of a principal's tacit knowledge that becomes explicitly available is significantly greater when conversations about one's practices are a central part of one's network participation and when opportunities are provided for demonstrating one's practices and responding to colleagues about the nature of those practices.

LSA'S RESEARCH ABOUT THE CHARACTERISTICS OF EFFECTIVE LEADERSHIP NETWORKS

The fundamental assumptions outlined in the previous section speak to both the means and ends of leadership networks, like PLTs, designed to improve the individual and collective learning of their members. With these assumptions in mind, both of LSA's empirical studies to date about PLTs addressed two questions: What are the characteristics of effective leadership networks? and What is the relative contribution to members' learning of their network engagement?

Both studies were guided by a framework or model of network effectiveness developed from an extensive review of research. Figure 9.1, summarizing this framework, proposes a set of causal relationships among five constructs.

FIGURE 9.1 Framework Guiding the Study

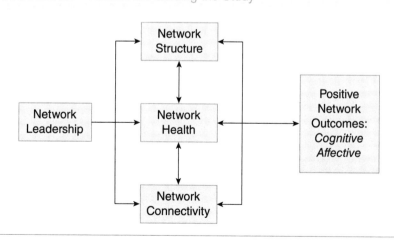

Network leadership influences the other three network concepts: *structure*, *health*, and *connectivity*. These three variables interact with one another, and the status or condition of these characteristics account for variation in both cognitive and affective *network outcomes*. Not all network outcomes are either intended or desirable, however.

The review of prior research undertaken to develop this broad framework also identified more specific characteristics of each of the variables in Figure 9.1. These more specific characteristics served as hypotheses to be tested by the two studies:

- *Network leadership:* effective leadership in networks is widely shared, helps develop clear purposes and focus, monitors network progress, and provides support of various sorts to network members.

- *Network health:* a healthy network is one that has explicit purpose and clear expectations, effective communication mechanisms, and both collaborative environments and trusting relationships.

- *Network structure:* both the size of the network (influenced by the typical ways in which members interact) and some member characteristics influence a network's effectiveness.

- *Network connectivity:* a network in which members are effectively connected includes frequent interactions among members and provides members with ready access to both local knowledge and external expertise when needed.

- *Network outcomes:* the first study focused on the individual professional capacity development of network members while the second study added a set of collective outcomes. Capacity was conceptualized as having both cognitive (e.g., refining one's school improvement skills) and affective (job satisfaction commitment, self-efficacy) components.

The first empirical study guided by this framework was completed during the 2014–15 school year, and the follow-up replication of that study was completed during the 2015–16 school year. Although the second study was labeled a replication, it included several features arising from the results of the first study, for example, the addition of a set of collective outcomes to the solely individual outcomes included in the first study, an expanded conception and measure of network leadership, and additional measures of network health focused on the "dark side" of collaboration.

Results of both studies largely confirmed the contribution of many of the characteristics in the framework to the further development of individual members' professional capacities—both cognitive and affective. In particular, network leadership, health, and connectivity accounted for large proportions of the variation in outcomes explained by the framework. As a whole, the framework explained about half of the variation in network outcomes.[1]

Results of the two studies produced three guidelines for LSA's Steering Team and members engaged in PLTs.

Knowledge Mobilization

LSA should provide those interested in improving the effectiveness of their networks with an opportunity to learn more about the results of this study and the implications it might have for their own networks.

Network Leadership Development

Substantial resources are now devoted to developing single-unit leadership. Unless systematic initiatives are also undertaken to further develop the capacities needed for effective network leadership, the significant time and money spent on leadership networks in districts is likely to have disappointing results. Such initiatives should help prepare network leaders to foster the forms of collaboration described in the study as central to professional capacity development.

Network Health

The studies describe not only the conditions that foster collaborative learning in leadership networks but also the conditions

---

[1] A detailed report of the first study can be found in Leithwood and Azah (2016).

that stand in the way of such learning (referred to in the study as the "dark side" of collaboration—for example, "groupthink"). Network leaders should systematically monitor and ameliorate "dark-side" conditions, as well as explicitly encourage those conditions that foster collaborative learning outlined in the study.

Network Structure and Connectivity

Those responsible for designing and/or leading networks are advised to keep the size of face-to-face networks fairly small (e.g., about a dozen members) and to ensure access to suitable, knowledge-building technology for larger networks.

A Story About a Productive Leadership Network[2]

This is the story of our learning journey as members of the District School Board of Niagara's LSA principal learning team. For the past eight years, administrators in the District School Board of Niagara (DSBN) have learned together through principal learning teams, or networks as they are called in the DSBN. Principals and vice principals fortunate enough to have been involved with Niagara's LSA team have had the added benefit of learning and growing with LSA members from across the province. We have had the opportunity to engage in knowledge building through provincial sessions with educational leaders like Ken Leithwood, Michael Fullan, and John Hattie and through district learning with Steven Katz, coauthor of *Intentional Interruption*. Our LSA planning sessions have provided a forum for discussing the ideas, research, and practices that build capacity in us as leaders and invite us to creatively and thoughtfully infuse them in our own practices.

Learning together has allowed us to ask questions that may not have come to us as individuals, for example, "What does this new knowledge mean to us? What will it look like in our buildings, and how can it positively impact student achievement? What does a coherent instructional guidance system look like

[2]This story was written by Christine Waler, Shelley Fehrman, Wes Hahn, Kristen Kosh, Megan Milani, Linda Oakes, Melanie Sendzik, Steve Webb, and Mary Zwolak. Reproduced with permission.

at the district level? What does meaningful learning look like? How do we balance direct instruction with a constructivist approach? How do we promote an inquiry stance in our schools and system? How do we balance informed prescription with informed professional judgment, knowing that informed prescription will take a school system only so far?"

Both experienced and newer members of Niagara's LSA team credit the LSA initiative with propelling our learning to places we would not have ventured on our own. Linda Oakes, principal of Oakwood Public School in Port Colborne, believes that the LSA experience has changed her participation in network meetings; she now makes a conscious effort to bring the new knowledge and experiences into her conversations, questions, and inquiries. She has learned that the network meeting must be a place for honest conversations about her wonderings, her struggles, and her leadership. She needs to leave each meeting with a plan for her next learning and with more to think about. Linda has learned that a principal learning team must have a collective sense of responsibility for the learning of all members, not just on the day of the network meeting but on all of the days in between. Participation in the LSA team has provided Linda with new experiences that have challenged her thinking, pushed her out of her comfort zone, and led her to truly believe that leadership makes a difference to all learners–teachers, parents, and students.

As a "rookie," Kristen Kosh, principal of Edith Cavell Public School in St. Catharines, thinks, metaphorically, about the LSA team as an iceberg. She views individuals on the team as the tip of the iceberg but collectively, under the surface, as a massive wealth of professional knowledge and inquiry. The LSA network has allowed her to reflect on her own practice and priorities as an administrator, her non-negotiables, so to speak. Having the opportunity to discuss research, question other people's interpretations, and truly dive into the work of today's most influential educational experts has profoundly built her own professional capacity, thereby influencing a change in priorities to better reflect the areas of need in her school. Through LSA, Kristen has experienced the value of a high-functioning principal learning team and the influence it can have on her, both personally and professionally, at the school level. It has led her to question what it is that makes a team "high functioning" and how to transfer the learning to the school level.

(Continued)

(Continued)

Shelley Fehrman, principal of Grapeview Public School in St. Catharines, believes that the work of the LSA team has resulted in an explosion of learning. Bringing a different lens from each area of our district, members of the LSA team build knowledge together by asking challenging questions and reflecting on the responses. The resulting synergy has translated into dramatic changes in Shelley's network practice, ultimately leading to changes in her school.

Mary Zwolak, principal of Westmount Public School in St. Catharines, credits the LSA initiative with bringing powerful practices to our board, including the "Bump It Up" strategy and John Hattie's research on what works best, including the high impact of timely and specific feedback.

Megan Milani, principal of Sheridan Park Public School in St. Catharines, believes that her LSA experience has been the best professional learning she has had as an administrator. She calls it a "gift." Within the LSA team, she has learned how to ask good questions and support answers with evidence. She has also learned the importance of staying with a problem of practice until it is clearly identified before moving on to a theory of action. Her understanding of inquiry-based learning has deepened, and the opportunity to reflect has led both to personal discomfort and exhilaration.

Steve Webb, principal of Garrison Road Public School in Fort Erie, points to the impact LSA's theory of action has had on network practices within the DSBN, specifically with respect to effective questioning. His experience with LSA has led to the realization that getting to the right question is the most important purpose of network learning.

Christine Waler, principal of Jacob Beam Public School in Beamsville, believes that the LSA experience has led to exponential growth in her leadership practices because of the opportunity to work with like-minded individuals in a culture of learning and knowledge building. She also credits the opportunity to participate in focused learning sessions with colleagues from around the province with challenging her thinking about effective leadership practices. Visits to schools, such as the Dr. Eric Jackman Institute for Child Studies, have affirmed the importance of a balanced approach to instruction that includes direct teaching, as well as inquiry. In recent years, the LSA experience, combined with purposeful network practices within the DSBN, have provided her with opportunities to clearly reflect on her role as lead learner in the school. It has also enabled her to zero in on her "real" challenges of practice through the many lenses provided by her colleagues.

Melanie Sendzik, principal of Riverview Public School in Niagara Falls, has participated in network learning in the DSBN for the past six years. She remembers the shift in her thinking about leadership when she was asked in her principal learning team, "What intentional leadership practices did you engage in to make that happen?"

The focus on what a leader specifically does to impact change in her or his school is in marked contrast to the "bring and brag" origins of principal learning teams in the DSBN. In the early days of our eight-year journey, principal learning teams were primarily focused on reporting and sharing school initiatives and their effects on student learning. Membership in networks was based on similar demographics, a common instructional focus, the province's School Effectiveness Framework, school size, or any number of other factors. Initially, meetings resembled book studies, and a culture of niceness often presented a barrier to deep learning. Over time, with the help of Steven Katz, we learned to refine the approach to our challenges of practice with effective questioning within a collaborative inquiry framework.

Currently, principal learning teams in the DSBN focus on administrator learning needs through the inquiry process. Our "class" is the teachers in our schools. A framework guides our thinking. Our goal for every meeting is to leave with our next best learning focus and our next best action. Our goal between meetings is to support each other in our schools. In a profound way, we have come to understand that none of us can do this alone. We continue to reflect on the purpose of our principal learning teams and have differentiated the structure and format within our district to reflect the needs of members. We have also come to understand the importance of having a "knowledgeable other" to guide and challenge our thinking. Coherence in our district has grown, largely through the questions that challenge our assumptions.

For Megan Milani, the network is so much more than a meeting. It is a group of professionals there to help each other on a learning journey in a real and purposeful way. Through principal learning teams in the DSBN, Mary Zwolak has come to understand that we will practice differently when we understand

(Continued)

(Continued)

differently and that the learning is the work. At times, the journey has been painstaking; however, the time invested has paid off. Frequently our colleagues describe leaving a network meeting feeling completely renewed or completely disturbed. We have come to understand that shifting one's thinking, either in our own work as leaders or with teachers in our schools, sometimes necessitates a compelling disturbance introduced at an opportune moment. Sometimes, the work is messy and uncomfortable. It is always challenging.

Wes Hahn, superintendent of schools in the DSBN, currently leads DSBN's principal learning team. In October 2012, our group attended the LSA symposium where Ken Leithwood outlined LSA's theory of action and the impact the Four Paths of Leadership Influence can have on student learning. As a team, we reflected on Leithwood's presentation, the goals of the LSA initiative, and our journey through eight years of principal learning teams in the District School Board of Niagara. We felt that we had reached the point in our journey where we could positively impact the learning in other school districts. During the symposium, we connected with principals and district leaders from both the Grand Erie District School Board and the Hamilton-Wentworth District School Board with the hope of sharing promising practices and developing leadership networks across districts in the province.

We discussed the possibilities of working as Tri-Board group and decided to focus on how we approach learning in principal learning teams. All three boards had invested time and expertise into making leadership network experiences both authentic and meaningful. Each board hosted a session, taking the group through its own network challenge of practice, highlighting key steps and strategies to ensure meaningful learning. The DSBN constructed a "fishbowl" activity where our LSA Network modeled for the other boards our process for digging into a principal's challenge of practice using the inquiry framework in our principal learning teams.

This was an extremely powerful experience for everyone. The trust and vulnerability of the people in the network were key to the success of the demonstration. It was an opportunity for everyone to reflect on their own board practices, ask questions, and formulate next steps back in their own district. For Megan Milani, the Tri-Board experience led to an increased understanding of the inquiry model, particularly around the importance of building trust, finding the challenge of practice through good questioning, supporting statements with evidence, and becoming more effective as a facilitator. For Linda Oakes, the Tri-Board experience led to a common understanding of how to positively impact student achievement. It reaffirmed the notion that we are not in this alone and that network learning can and should be about the leader's learning. For Shelley Fehrman, the Tri-Board experience fundamentally changed her practice in her school. The result for all three districts has been a synergy of learning and growing. Recently, Lakehead District School Board has joined our networked learning journey.

The LSA team in Niagara has had the opportunity to participate in a four-board learning initiative with Grand Erie, Hamilton-Wentworth, and now Lakehead; twice presented our network journey at a provincial symposium in Toronto; written an article for the OPC *Register*; participated in LSA webinars; and flown to Thunder Bay to share our journey. This year, we are looking more deeply into focused instruction and have returned to Hattie's research to guide our learning.

While this is the story of the DSBN's LSA journey and the potential of principal learning teams to impact student achievement, interwoven in these words are the stories of many principals in the province who, through their LSA experiences, have emerged as brighter, more empowered, and more inspired leaders. The LSA project has succeeded in building capacity in principals across the province to be the leaders who can and will create the conditions in their schools for all learners to reach their potential—and that is everyone's story!

CONCLUSION

This chapter described the evolution of leadership networks (or principal learning teams) in districts supported by the LSA project. LSA provided an early stimulus for districts to form PLTs. Further development of PLTs continued, in no small measure, because of ongoing evidence from PLT members, over about a decade, about the contribution such networks made to their professional growth.

Prompted by the accumulation of such persistent findings, LSA then began its own research about the features of effective networks in order to provide additional guidance to project members about how to get even more out of their network experiences. As the story about network learning in one district illustrated, principal learning teams have become hubs for transforming tacit into explicit knowledge and for collaborative inquiry about a wide range of problems of practice, including how to implement many of LSA's other programs and practices in individual members' schools.

It also seems likely that productive leadership networks, such as the one featured in the story, build trust among a district's school leaders that pay off in many ways that are not entirely predictable; they are likely the most powerful sources of leadership learning that a district can nurture. Evidence from LSA's research and experience suggests, in addition, that well-functioning leadership networks provide considerable autonomy to members in deciding what is considered worth learning, prompt members to consider new ideas from their influential peers, offer members concrete examples of effective leadership practices, and provide the types of social persuasion, modeling, and mastery experiences associated with improvements in leaders' individual and collective efficacy.

Chapter 10

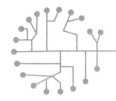

INSIGHTS ABOUT LEADING LARGE-SCALE LEADERSHIP DEVELOPMENT PROJECTS

At the time of this writing (spring 2017), the LSA project is just completing its twelfth year. This is a remarkable length of time to sustain almost any consistent change effort in education, especially one that has remained a "project" for its entire life. This chapter explores the most plausible reasons for such success and offers potentially useful insights or lessons to others responsible for large-scale leadership development. As with all things LSA, the starting point for insights in this chapter have been developed from the best available evidence, which, in this case, comes from those who have led the project from its inception. In February 2012 and again in the late spring of 2014, the project evaluator conducted focus group interviews with LSA's Steering Team members. A review of the results of those two focus group interviews by the Steering Team in early 2017 concluded that those results remained a faithful representation of its current views.

In the case of both focus group interviews, data were collected over a period of about two hours, with most of the Steering Team members in attendance. The interviews were guided by a broad set of questions that launched fairly extended conversations among team members. These conversations were periodically interrupted with follow-up questions from the interviewer. Interviews were audio recorded, and extensive notes were also taken during the interviews. This chapter is a synthesis of results from the two focus group interviews, as well as additional interpretations of their meaning prompted by related research.

The remainder of the chapter consists of three sections. The first section shines a light on four of the most significant practical challenges LSA has faced, along with implications for others to consider as they take their own projects forward. Titled "One Big Technical Challenge," the second section compares LSA approach to assessing its effects on students with the most likely alternatives. The final section surfaces eleven lessons about leading large-scale leadership development. While none of these implications and lessons, by themselves, is new, pulling them together in this one final chapter makes especially clear what we think others can learn from our experience.

FOUR PRACTICAL CHALLENGES IN SUSTAINING LSA

A central theme ran through Steering Team members' responses to the focus groups' interview questions. This was the team's *modus operandi*—one of learning from the challenges, adapting the project in response to evidence of several types about what was working and what was not moving the project in a desired direction. This *modus operandi* required considerable patience, persistence, and resilience on the part of Steering Team members but appears to be the central explanation for the progress that has been made through the project to date. Responding carefully and relatively quickly to challenges as they arose is a key explanation for the project's success. What were those challenges also likely to be encountered by others doing similar work? The Steering Team respondents identified four sets of such challenges, each of which contains potential implications for others. Be forewarned.

While the project pursued an evolving stream of initiatives with considerable potential for helping leaders improve their students' achievement, actually implementing those initiatives in members' schools turned out to be complex, as was supporting principals in developing the capacities they needed to lead such implementation. The complexity of actual implementation appeared to be a function of having to work from incomplete knowledge, adapt to local circumstances, and help members see the alignment among multiple, sometimes seemingly disparate, efforts.

First, it was clear from LSA's annual evaluations that increasing a school's academic press, for example, held considerable promise for improving the achievement of its students. But actually bringing about such an increase in academic press was the complicated part—and the part about which there was the least codified knowledge on which to draw (e.g., Goddard, Sweetland, & Hoy, 2000); such incomplete knowledge is hardly unique to academic press. Second, finding the most productive balance between encouraging the implementation of project initiatives with enough fidelity to realize their benefits and adapting those initiatives to project members' needs and reactions was an ongoing and sometime elusive job for project members; this challenge has been recognized by research on change dating back many years (Berman & McLaughlin, 1978). Finally, the evolving nature of the project's priorities meant that Steering Team leaders were faced with a constant demand to keep its many moving parts aligned in service of its overall purpose, especially in the minds of participants. Such alignment, evidence suggests, is critical to members' sense making (Brown, Stacey, & Nandhakumar, 2007).

The LSA experience suggests that those planning their own large-scale leadership development projects should assign a large proportion of their resources to supporting members' implementation of project priorities. Resources used to implement many educational innovations are often front-end loaded with diminishing resources available for solving what are predictably the most complex problems facing implementers downstream.

Communication Challenges

From the outset, it proved challenging to create effective ways of communicating with project members in order to keep them informed about project activities and to receive timely feedback from them. With experience, the Steering Team got much better at such communication, making increasingly extensive use of information technology, for example, mass e-mails to participants through the three principals' associations, and much greater use of web-based/online resources. The Steering Team members were also in quite regular contact with one another.

Especially in the early years of the project, realizing the potential of electronic technology for communication with and among project members was much more difficult than it was later, although this challenge has not yet been fully overcome. One longtime Steering Team member, for example, reflected on the steep learning curve for many of those on the Steering Team required by the project's early efforts to make more extensive use of the available technology. Crucial support was provided by the information technology specialist on the team as project members worked at using this technology for the first time.

While uses of information technology continued to expand rapidly from those early days, an expansion similar to what occurred in the New Leaders program (Gates et al., 2014), Steering Team members with this responsibility point to the significantly greater demands this has placed on their time and resources. Any large-scale leadership development project should plan for multiple ways of keeping project members and leaders in close contact.

Challenges Arising From Changing Personnel

Over the project's history, there has been constant change in LSA's membership, mostly through the addition of significant numbers of new members each year, with very few departures. This constant membership increase presented the Steering Team with two problems. One problem was how to accommodate additional members with few additional resources. The second problem was how to differentiate the services required to effectively support the development of those new to the project, those who had participated in the project for many years, and all those in between.

Even without constantly growing membership, a significant challenge was to suitably differentiate the support provided to project participants given their different levels of experiences (e.g., first-year principals, principals with lengthy experience) and work contexts (e.g., school size, district support). One Steering Team member noted, for example, that it was increasingly harder to find symposium speakers who "hit the mark" for all or most of the LSA participants. Other examples included variation among LSA participants in their readiness for deep conversations about practice among themselves and the readiness to take seriously the results of research to help guide practice. The implication of this challenge for others embarking on large-scale leadership development projects is to build in orientation opportunities for new members and provide some differentiation of support for existing participants.

A constantly changing Steering Team membership has been a much less demanding challenge. At the time of this writing, about half the Steering Team's members have been on the team since the beginning of the project (including the chair of the Steering Committee) while the other half were more recent. The core of members, those with the project since its inception, or close to it, have acted as the project's organizational memory. New members have mostly been sources of fresh perspectives and new ideas, helping to keep the project responsive to the changing policy and practice contexts in the province. ("They asked good questions that we hadn't thought of," noted one interviewee.) Furthermore, all new Steering Team members have agreed from the outset with the central goal of the project and have been highly motivated to help ensure its continuing success. The Steering Team chair has provided exceptionally skillful coordination, facilitation, and follow-through on decisions made during Steering Team meetings.

What motivates the Steering Team and the participating principals of the LSA project to sustain their collective leadership endeavors? A possible answer can be found in the words of Lieberman and Grolnick (1996):

> When networks, coalitions, and partnerships last long enough to create ongoing learning communities, cultures based on mutual knowledge, learning, and collaboration replace the transmission of knowledge from one institution to another. These cultures, focused on critical issues of

school reform, place educational practice at their centre, providing the kind of social and professional nourishment that leads many members to invest time, effort, and commitment far beyond what they give to the usual professional development organizations. (p. 41)

Challenges Arising From Expansion Into Secondary Schools

The LSA project began in elementary schools and remained with that organizational focus for the first three years. Many of its early priorities were established with this elementary focus in mind. Beginning to include secondary schools into the project demanded significant modifications in the project's main thrusts as well as an expansion of Steering Team capacities to manage such modifications. Not all of these efforts were successful, and the expansion to secondary schools has been very demanding. But this expansion added considerable weight to the project and resulted in additional Steering Team capacity. Much has been learned from the addition of secondary schools.

Challenges associated with LSA's move into secondary schools reflect a significant amount of prior evidence, indicating that secondary school responses to change are quite different from responses to change in elementary schools—for example, Louis and Lee's (2016) research about the extent to which teachers' professional cultures influence the capacity of teachers to respond productively to new information, that is, to engage in organizational learning. Core features of professional cultures, conceptualized and measured in that study as including academic press, academic support for students, and trust and respect, had a strong influence on teachers' organizational learning. However, these qualities diminished with school level, as did teachers' capacities for organizational learning.

There is at least one implication for other leadership developers of the challenge presented by LSA's extension into secondary schools. Leadership development projects intending to serve secondary school leaders would be advised to explicitly take account of the well-documented responses to change of secondary schools and the consequences of those responses for effective secondary school leadership. A great deal of creative talent is required by principals and teachers to translate visions of improved education into effective means across elementary and secondary and varied linguistic and demographic contexts. Any instructional package that is not amenable to such productive variation and that requires "one size fit all" is unlikely to be successful for many of its participants. That is why LSA supports approaches amenable to creative local adaptation and innovation.

ONE LARGE TECHNICAL CHALLENGE: ASSESSING THE PROJECT'S IMPACT ON STUDENTS

This is the most technically complex of the challenges LSA encountered. While the LSA project has attracted very positive responses from almost all of its members, the project's formal evaluation eventually adopted an indirect method of assessing impact on students. The choice of student achievement, as a dependent variable for evaluating leadership development programs, may well be a "bridge too far" to be reasonable, as we explain later; it is, nevertheless, one that many insist on, including many program funders.

As Chapter 2 explained, after using a simple province-wide comparison of LSA and non-LSA participants' school achievement during the first two years of the project (and finding no differences), LSA adopted an indirect solution to the problem.[1] It is worth noting that evaluations of the National Institute of School Leadership (NISL) program failed to find any effects on student achievement until participants had been in their schools for at least several years.

One part of this solution was to assess the local impact of LSA's priorities (not schools) on student achievement. The second part of the solution was to develop qualitative case studies (real stories) of LSA's contribution to the development of individual schools and districts. This combination of indirect quantitative and direct

---

[1] It is worth noting that Nunnery, Ross, and Yen (2010a, 2010b) evaluation of the National Institute for School Leadership Executive Development did not detect any effects on the achievement of students in participants' schools until the third year after attending the program.

qualitative evidence seems to have satisfied most of the project's stakeholders.

Assessing the impact on student achievement of program participants is likely to be a challenge for most large-scale leadership development projects, and LSA's solution may be a hard sell. Project funders, for example, may expect the kind of evaluation designs used in the small number of mostly recent evaluations that have used student achievement as outcome measures. Examples of programs assessed in this way include the New Leaders program (Gates et al., 2014), the National Institute for School Leadership Executive Development Program (Nunnery et al., 2010a, 2010b) and the Greater New Orleans School Leadership Center program (Leithwood, Riedlinger, & Bauer, 2003). These evaluations use approximations to experimental or quasi-experimental research designs, including a treatment group that receives the program and a control or matching group that receives whatever crops up in its environment (what Jacob, Goddard, Kim, Miller, & Goddard, 2015, refer to as "business as usual"). The assumptions underlying the use of such designs are often very difficult to meet, however, and this is one of several explanations for LSA moving in a different direction.

One assumption is that the features of the program being evaluated are relatively stable and well defined. Absent such clarity and stability, the cause of the treatment group's effects on students will be unknowable. Nunnery et al.'s (2010a, 2010b) evaluation of the NISL Executive Development Program, for example, benefited from at least some degree of specification, as did Leithwood et al.'s (2003) evaluation of the Greater New Orleans School Leadership Center program. In contrast, Gates et al.'s (2014) finding of significant effects on student achievement after three years of participation in the New Leaders program is difficult to interpret because the program continued to evolve in a manner reminiscent of LSA.

The LSA program has always been a work in progress. It has evolved as district and provincial priorities have evolved and the implementation of its priorities has been carried out, in most districts, in combination with other district-specific initiatives. LSA's program can be described in very general terms (see Chapter 4) but not in terms sufficiently specific or stable to meet the assumptions of an experimental or quasi-experimental evaluation design.

A second assumption underlying the use of an experimental or quasi-experimental evaluation design is that those receiving the program (the treatment group) and those not receiving the program (the control or matched group) have nonoverlapping professional learning experiences during the period of program implementation. This assumption can rarely be justified even when evaluating very well specified programs. For example, Jacob et al.'s (2015) evaluation of McREL's Balanced Leadership Program found substantial overlap between the content and learning experiences of those assigned to the treatment and control groups during the time the McREL program was being implemented. Most districts provide some form of ongoing professional development for their school leaders, and this professional development will often compete with the program being evaluated in terms of both content and impact. In such cases, leadership development experiences may well be making substantial contributions to student achievement, but it is difficult to determine which of those experiences matter most.

A third assumption underlying the use of experimental or quasi-experimental designs for evaluating leadership development programs is that any observed changes in student achievement are attributable to changes in the practices of program participants in their schools. However, there are many influences on what schools do "in play" at the same time, and changes in what leaders do is likely to account for only a portion of observed changes in student learning (Bryk, Bender Sebring, Allensworth, Leppescu, & Easton, 2010; Jacob et al., 2015). One of the reasons for such a modest expectation can be explained by the underlying theory of action assumed by these experimental or quasi-experimental evaluation designs—some close version of the following:

1. The new capacities (knowledge, skill, dispositions) specified in the curriculum of the leadership development program have the potential to improve conditions in schools with significant impact on student learning.

2. Leaders participating in the program will acquire the new capacities specified in the program's curriculum.

3. Having acquired these new capacities, participants will change their actual practices in their schools in reflection of the new capacities.

4. The changed leadership practices in program members' schools will lead to changes in one or more school conditions experienced directly by students.

5. Changes in one or more of these school conditions will lead to improved learning opportunities for students.

6. Students will avail themselves of these new learning opportunities and this will improve their performance on whatever measures of student achievement are used by the program evaluation.

None of these six assumptions can be taken for granted. With respect to the first assumption, for example, there is only weak consensus in the research community about what leadership capacities are most worth learning (e.g., Leithwood, 2012; Robinson, Lloyd, & Rowe, 2008). About the third assumption, Jacob et al. (2015), for example, found very uneven actual use in schools of the capacities principals claimed to have acquired through their participation in McREL's Balanced Leadership Program.

So unless an evaluation collects data confirming each of the six assumptions (we know of no such evaluation), the findings of an experimental or quasi-experimental study can easily result in a conclusion, for example, that (a) the leadership development program had no significant effect on student achievement when, in fact, the capacities it aimed to develop were not actually implemented by participants in sufficient degree or (b) the capacities developed through the leadership program had significant effects on students when something else was responsible (e.g., teachers in participants' schools were persuaded to do things differently by the symbolic act of their principal's enrollment in the program).

The exceedingly modest achievement results teased out by Rand's lengthy and methodologically robust evaluation of the extensively promoted New Leaders program (Gates et al., 2014) suggests that designing evaluations capable of ruling out the effects of all but the leadership development project are, if not extremely difficult to create, at least inordinately expensive to implement. Designing evaluations to detect the effects on students of well-developed, long-standing leadership development programs remains an outstanding challenge.

ELEVEN LESSONS ABOUT
EFFECTIVE PROJECT LEADERSHIP

The lessons discussed in this section can be found sprinkled through other chapters of the book; they are brought together here in order to clarify what can be learned from LSA by those responsible for other large-scale leadership development projects. Unsurprisingly, these lessons are neither independent of one another nor of the five challenges appearing in the previous section.

1. **Appreciate the Complexities of Large-scale Improvement Processes**

   The Steering Team has developed a very refined appreciation of the complexities associated with effecting significant improvement across many schools and has adopted a patient, incremental approach to the change process. This process starts with the selection of a "promising" (based on carefully weighing the available evidence) addition to its repertoire of interventions, then supports its introduction in project schools by providing principals with opportunities to acquire whatever new capacities implementing the initiative might require, proactively monitoring such implementation, and making whatever adjustments or refinements seem called for by the feedback. Experience in the project emphasizes the importance of being responsive to the feedback and reactions of participants, as distinct from designing and implementing a "canned" approach to the project.

2. **Align Leadership Development With the Larger Reform Initiatives**

   Evolution of the project has been organic and in line with directions taken by the province, as a whole. So participants view their work in the project as not only consistent with provincial and district directions but as helpful in pursuing those broader directions in their own school contexts. Although the project is intended primarily to support principals' efforts, its work has gradually been extended to those central office leaders who work with principals in their own districts. This helps ensure that district and LSA initiatives remain aligned and that project participants do not become isolated from their system colleagues as they pursue project initiatives in their own schools.

Participants are able to view the project work as their school and district work. Similarly, the Ministry of Education's representation on the Steering Team also helps ensure alignment of project and ministry priorities.

3. **Be Persistent and Resilient**

The change process, as described earlier, assumes considerable persistence on the part of the Steering Team acting as a change agent. From the beginning of the project (with its early emphasis on professional learning communities), when LSA priorities did not have the initial impact anticipated for them, the Steering Team did not give up on them. Rather, the team worked at determining the reasons for the lack of impact and persevering "as long as it took" until the initiatives either made the contribution they were originally selected to make or had clearly demonstrated their limits. This perseverance, persistence, and resilience have become key features of the Steering Team's "modus operandi" and models a key set of dispositions required by school and district leaders in their own improvement efforts. Even the most well-developed and evidence-based initiatives rarely realize their potential without considerable "adaptive" effort by those implementing them.[2]

4. **Adopt a "Learning Mindset"**

The Steering Team has behaved as a learning organization using the evidence available to it to build knowledge and "think outside the box," unconstrained by an overabundance of bureaucracy. New members joining the Steering Team join a strong learning culture—a culture significantly reinforced by the careful written record of the project's history, initiatives, and effects. This mindset is contagious; it has been "caught" by many participants as a result of their experiences with LSA initiatives. As principals worked on LSA initiatives in their schools, they gained new skills and gained confidence in their own abilities to lead change. These new skills and disposition, in turn, created new possibilities for what the Steering Team could aspire to at the next stage of its work. So the team learned to "learn its way forward" and became a better collective problem solver, as a

---

[2]This lesson was first documented in the late 1970s by Berman and McLaughlin (1978) in their landmark study of innovation implementation in schools.

result. This mindset seems a productive one to adopt, no matter the project, and is very much a part of the first two lessons (identified previously).

5. **Make the Project's Value Self-Evident**

A project like LSA has to be seen to have value and credibility for advancing a set of shared goals if people are going to willingly participate in it. LSA's location and leadership in the province's three principal associations added considerably to its perceived value, building on the trust and credibility principals already awarded their own professional associations. Collaboration required among the three principals' associations to lead the project helped to further cooperation among these associations on other matters. The project also was able to make use of, add to, and validate much of the other professional development typically provided by the province's three principals' associations to its members. The project has benefited from access to the databases and other resources already assembled in the three associations.

Engagement of LSA with principals—and more recently with central office leaders—has encouraged a culture of "collective leadership" in the province by clarifying the practical meaning of "tri-level leadership," for example. This culture is a source of encouragement for others in schools and districts to move through leadership positions and so contributes to leadership succession efforts in the province.

6. **Foster Relationships and Build Trust**

While by no means a new insight, the multiple organizations cooperating in support of the LSA project demonstrate the value of trusting relationships in getting good work done. Furthermore, each of the Steering Team members is also trusted by the members of their own organizations, some of whom are part of the LSA project. Trusting relationships are usually not sufficient for project success, but they are almost always necessary.

Efforts to encompass the views and interests of leaders at many levels of the system have also broadened team members' understanding of how to go about improvement on a large scale.

The project has become a way for participants, within and across school systems, to connect with, collaborate, and learn from one another. Opportunities for these connections and the learning they allow have been gradually enhanced by the digital supports provided by the project. While use of these supports was slow to develop, they are now viewed as increasingly important, in part because they, too, have evolved in response to participant feedback and research.

The project has modeled a flatter, more democratic form of leadership, one consistent with a model of "authentic" leadership and one that listens to and honors many voices, both complementary and critical voices.

7. **Engage in Regular and Frequent Monitoring**

The value of establishing monthly meetings of the Steering Team to monitor progress and consider new or revised priorities indicates the importance for project leadership of being very "hands on." It is much easier to address problems in their early stages of development than it is after they have had a chance to mature. Participants also know their voices are being heard, and the project embodies a culture that respects and acknowledges those voices. Steering Team members consult with participants informally "behind the scenes" and formally through various instruments to keep informed about participants' challenges and successes.

8. **Make Project Membership Invitational**

Membership in the project is "invitational." Over the life span of the project, to date, there has been significant growth in membership. In most cases, the motivation to join has seemed to come from a growing reputation among leaders in the province that participation in the project will help them with their work. New members are treated with respect, and significant efforts are made to support new members, no matter their starting points. This seems a productive approach to the leadership and management of many projects and suggests "going to scale" by being irresistible rather than autocratic.

9. **Pay Unwavering Attention to the Same Goal**

The project has never lost its focus on improving student achievement by improving school leadership as its primary goal and has been guided by research in refining how that goal can best be achieved. While this goal has remained constant, the means by which this goal is accomplished have evolved considerably in response to evidence about what is working well in participants' schools and what is not.

10. **Use Evidence to Ensure the Integrity of Decisions**

The LSA project is considered by most of its participants as having considerable integrity. The project directions and priorities are taken especially seriously because they are arrived at transparently through the careful analysis of both project-generated evidence and evidence from the wider research community. Results of the ongoing project evaluation are primary sources of the evidence used by the Steering Team in its decisions.

11. **Be Careful What You Wish For (or the Virtues of "Project" Status)**

After a few years of success, it is not unusual for many project leaders to actively aspire to and advocate for their project to be awarded more permanent status in the organization, especially in the organization's budget. But indefinite project status has advantages not to be dismissed lightly. Projects are typically characterized by, for example, specific goals, challenging timelines, close monitoring of initiatives, expectations of explicit evidence of success, and freedom to work outside at least some of the boundaries of established practices and procedures. Features such as these often stimulate special interest and enthusiasm among those involved; project work is not just about "business as usual." These features and others were also part of the LSA project and help account for some of LSA's effects. For example, LSA has been compelled to learn from the challenges it faced or go out of business. Adopting a responsive disposition toward these challenges has enhanced the quality and impact of the project. There have been significant "midcourse adjustments." And as one Steering Team member said, "the challenges made us more creative"; another noted that the challenges "took us out of our comfort zone." Indeed, one of the most promising explanations for the successes experienced in the project to date is the resiliency demonstrated by the Steering Team.

Nimbleness is another feature of project status. Because LSA is a "project" rather than a branch of government or an initiative for which a branch of government has day-to-day responsibility and control, there have been fewer "hoops to jump through"; the project stands apart from many of the controls and regulations often associated with an initiative belonging to "the bureaucracy." As a consequence, the project can be very "nimble" when necessary.

LSA's project status has also provided it with access to resources from multiple sources. The project is carried out through the three provincial principals' associations and is sponsored by several divisions within the ministry. This has meant that the project also has had access to many of the resources associated with all of these organizations, a much greater set of potential resources than would be available if the project were an initiative of only one of these organizations.

While consistent in its goal with both district and provincial directions, many participants in the project have also developed a sense of community with their project colleagues. The project was initiated during a time in the province when many principals felt little autonomy over their own professional development. From the outset, as one of the project founders noted, LSA was conceptualized as a "collaborative," an initiative "owned" by those who participated in it. This ownership has, no doubt, had much to do with the sense of community experienced by many project members. The project promised them a voice in their own development; it also has taken them outside the formal organizations in which they work, brought them into contact with peers from outside their own districts, expanding their professional networks, and has been free from the sense of hierarchy that some feel in their own schools and districts.

CONCLUSION

The two focus group interviews with the LSA Steering Team and Board paint an optimistic picture of project contributions to participants' professional work and offer important insights about what it takes to develop the professional capital of school leaders on a large scale. After Hargreaves and Fullan (2012), professional capital is the combined total of human capital (individual capacity), social capital (the capacity that emerges from interaction within a group) and decisional capital (bringing human and social capital to bear on the exercise of choice).

The LSA project has provided many opportunities for individual leaders to refine their leadership skills and knowledge. Through principal learning teams, for example, the project has also helped create and support networks of school and system leaders who, at their best, know more about how to do productive school improvement work than any one participant does alone. As well—and without being prescriptive—the LSA theory of action has helped participants avoid wasting time and resources by narrowing the focus of their school improvement decisions to "key learning conditions" that evidence indicates make a demonstrable difference to the achievement of their students.

Accomplishments of this order are rare and certainly do not come easily. They require inordinate amounts of persistence, a willingness to learn on the fly, high levels of respect for good evidence and an unwavering commitment to the overarching goal of the project. Such accomplishments also depend on high levels of sensitivity to local aspirations and the circumstances faced by project participants. As the results of the two focus group interviews indicate, the LSA Steering Team and Board have been successful because of the high levels of professional capital they have developed and sustained, even as their individual members have gradually and inevitably changed.

We believe the LSA story described in this book provides insights for many others engaged in the difficult and complex work not only of leadership development but educational reform more broadly. As one of our reviewers concluded, "the most useful feature of the book is the focus on a broadly applicable, high impact problem (school improvement . . .) and the elaboration of how research, practice, lived experience, evaluation and responses can cohere into what [is sometimes called] organizational learning systems" (Hallinger, 2017, personal communication).

REFERENCES

CHAPTER 1

Bryk, A., Gomez, L., & Grunow, A. (2011). *Getting ideas into action: Building networked improvement communities in education.* Stanford, CA: Carnegie Foundation for the Advancement of Teaching.

Chen, B., & Hong, H.-Y. (2016). Schools as knowledge-building organizations: Thirty years of design research. *Educational Psychologist, 51*(2), 266–288. doi:10.1080/00461520.2016.1175306

Creemers, B. P. M., & Reezigt, G. J. (1996). School level conditions affecting the effectiveness of instruction. *School Effectiveness and School Improvement, 7,* 197–228.

Fullan, M. (2007). *The new meaning of educational change* (4th ed.). New York, NY: Teachers College Press.

Hallinger, P. (in press). Strategic instructional leadership: From prescription to theory to practice. In G. Hall, L. Quinn, & D. Gollnick (Eds.), *Handbook on teaching and learning.* New York, NY: Wiley-Blackwell.

Hallinger, P., & Heck, R. H. (1996). Reassessing the principal's role in school effectiveness: A review of empirical research, 1980–1995. *Educational Administration Quarterly, 32*(1), 5–44.

Huber, S., & West, M. (2002). Developing school leaders: A critical review of current practices, approaches and issues and some directions for the future, In K. Leithwood and P. Hallinger (Eds.) *Second International Handbook of Educational Leadership and Administration,* Dordrecht, The Netherlands, Kluwer Publishing, 1071–1101.

Leithwood, K. (2006). Leadership according to the evidence. *Leadership and Policy in Schools, 5*(3), 177–202.

Leithwood, K. (2012). *The Ontario Leadership Framework 2012 with a discussion of the research foundations.* Toronto, Canada: Institute for Educational Leadership

Leithwood, K., Harris, A., & Strauss, T. (2010). *Leading school turnaround: How successful leaders transform low-performing schools.* San Francisco, CA: Jossey-Bass.

Leithwood, K., & Jantzi, D. (1999). Transformational leadership effects: A replication. *School Effectiveness and School Improvement, 10*(4), 451–479.

Leithwood, K., Mascall, B., & Strauss, T. (2009). Distributed leadership: New perspectives on an old idea (Introduction). In K. Leithwood, B. Mascall, & T. Strauss (Eds.), *Distributed leadership according to the evidence* (pp. 1–14). New York, NY: Routledge.

Leithwood, K., & Menzies, T. (1998). Forms and effects of school-based management: A review. *Educational Policy, 12*(3), 325–346.

Leithwood, K., Riedlinger, B., Bauer, S., & Jantzi, D. (2003). Leadership program effects on student learning: The case of the Greater New Orleans School Leadership Center. *Journal of School Leadership, 13*(6), 707–738.

Leithwood, K., Seashore Louis, K., Wahlstrom, K., & Anderson, S. (2004). *Review of research: How leadership influences student learning.* New York, NY: Wallace Foundation.

Marzano, R. J., Waters, T., & McNulty, B. A. (2005). *School leadership that works.* Alexandria, VA: Association for Supervision and Curriculum Development.

Meindl, J. (1995). The romance of leadership as a follower-centric theory: A social constructivist approach. *Leadership Quarterly, 6*(3), 329–341.

Mourshed, M., Chijoke, C., & Barber, M. (2010). *How the world's most improved school systems keep getting better.* New York, NY: McKinsey and Company.

Ontario Ministry of Education. (2005). *Achieving excellence: A renewed vision for education in Ontario.* Toronto, Ontario: Author.

Pearce, C., & Conger, J. (2003). *Shared leadership: Reframing the hows and whys of leadership.* Thousand Oaks, CA: SAGE.

Peters, G. (1992). The policy process: An institutionalist perspective. *Canadian Public Administration, 35*(2), 160–180.

Pollock, K., Wang, F., & Hauseman, D. C. (2014). *The changing nature of principals' work: Final report.* Retrieved from http://www.edu.uwo.ca/faculty_profiles/cpels/pollock_katina/OPC-Principals-Work-Report.pdf

CHAPTER 2

Ball, A. (2012) To know is not enough: knowledge, power, and the zone of generativity. *Educational Researcher, 41*(8), 283–293.

Broekkamp, H., & van Hout-Walters, B. (2007). The gap between educational research and practice: A literature review, symposium and questionnaire. *Educational Research and Evaluation, 13*(3), 203–220.

Century, J., & Cassata, A. (2016). Implementing research: Finding common ground on what, how, why, where and who. *Review of Research in Education*, 40, 143–169.

CHAPTER 3

Australian Institute for Teaching and School Leadership. (2015). *Australian professional standard for principals and the leadership profiles.* Victoria: Education Services Australia.

Avey, J., Wernsing, T., & Luthans, F. (2008). Can positive employees help positive organizational change? Impact of psychological capital and emotions on relevant attitudes and behaviors, *The Journal of Applied Behavioral Science*, 44(1), 48–70.

Erdogan, B., &, Liden, R. (2002). Social exchanges in the workplace: A review of recent developments and future directions in leader–member exchange theory. In L. Neider & C. Schriesheim (Eds.), *Leadership* (pp. 65–114). Greenwich, CT: Information Age.

Hallinger, P. (2018). Bringing context out of the shadows of leadership. *Educational Management, Leadership and Administration*, 46(1), 5–24.

Hitt, D., & Tucker, P. (2016). Systematic review of key leadership practices found to influence student achievement: A unified framework. *Review of Educational Research*, 86, 531–569.

Leithwood, K. (1994). Leadership for school restructuring. *Educational Administration Quarterly*, 30, 498–518.

Leithwood, K. (2012). *The Ontario Leadership Framework with a discussion of the research foundations.* Toronto, Canada: Institute for Educational Leadership.

Leithwood, K., & Riehl, C. (2005). What do we already know about school leadership. In W. Firestone & C. Riehl (Eds.), *A new agenda for research in educational leadership* (pp. 12–27). New York, NY: Teachers College Press.

Leithwood, K., & Steinbach, R. (1995). *Expert problem solving: Evidence from school and district leaders.* New York, NY: SUNY Press.

Leithwood, K., Sun, J., & Pollock, K. (Eds.). *How successful Leaders contribute to student success: The four paths framework.* Switzerland: Kluwer International Publishing.

Mumford, M., Bedell, K., Hunter, S., Espejo, J., & Boatman, P. (2006). Problem-solving—turning crises into opportunities: How charismatic, ideological and pragmatic leaders solve problems. In M. Mulford (Ed.), *Handbook of organizational creativity* (pp. 108–137). Mahwah, NJ: Lawrence Earlbaum.

National College for School Leadership. (2008). *The national standards for school leadership: Consultation paper.* London, England: Department for Children, Schools and Families.

National Policy Board for Educational Administration. (2015). *Professional standards for educational leaders 2015.* Reston, VA: Author

Printy, S., Marks, H., & Bowers, A. (2010). *Integrated leadership: How principals and teachers share transformational and instructional influences.* East Lansing: Michigan State University.

Rowan, B., Fang-Shen, C., & Miller, R. (1997). Using research on employees' performance to student the effects of teachers on student achievement. *Sociology of Education, 70,* 256–284.

Sadri, G., Weber, T., & Gentry, W. (2011). Empathic emotions and leadership performance: An empirical analysis across 38 countries, *The Leadership Quarterly, 22,* 5, 818–830.

Waters, T., & Cameron, G. (2007). *The balanced leadership framework: Connecting vision with action.* Denver, CO: McREL.

Yukl, G. (1994). *Leadership in organizations* (3rd ed.). Englewood Cliffs, NJ: Prentice Hall.

Zacarro, S., Kemp, C., & Bader, P. (2004). Leader traits and abilities. In J. Antonakis, A. Cianciolo, & R. Sternberg (Eds.), *The nature of leadership* (pp. 104–124). Thousand Oaks, CA: SAGE.

CHAPTER 4

Berman, P., & McLaughlin, M. (1978). *Federal programs supporting educational change: implementing and sustaining innovations.* Santa Monica, CA: RAND Corporation

Century, J., & Cassata, A. (2016). Implementation research: Finding common ground on what, how, why, where and who. *Review of Education, 49,* 169–216.

Corcoran, R., Reilly, J., & Ross, S. (2015). *An examination of the effect of the National Institute for School Leadership's Executive Development Program on school performance trends in Milwaukee: A propensity score analysis.* Baltimore, MD: Johns Hopkins University.

Fullan, M. (2006). *Turnaround leadership.* Thousand Oaks, CA: Corwin.

Kindt, E., Gijbels, D., Grosemans, I., & Donch, V. (2016). Teachers' everyday professional development: Mapping informal learning activities, antecedents and learning outcomes. *Review of Educational Research, 86*(4), 1111–1150.

Makel, M., & Plucker, J. (2014). Facts are more important than novelty: Replication in the education sciences. *Educational Researcher, 43*(6), 304–316.

Miller, R., Goddard, R., Kim, M., Jacob, R., Goddard, Y., & Schroeder, P. (2016). Can professional development improve school leadership?

Results from a randomized control trial assessing the impact of McREL's Balanced Leadership Program on principals in rural Michigan schools. *Educational Administration Quarterly, 52*(4), 531–566.

Murphy, K., & Knight, S. (2016). Exploring a century of advancement in the science of learning. *Review of Research in Education, 40,* 402–456.

Rogoff, B., Callanan, M., Gutierrez, K., & Erickson, F. (2016). The organization of informal learning. *Review of Research in Education, 40,* 356–401.

Winn, K. M., Anderson, E., Groth, C., Korach, S., Pounder, D., Rorrer, A. & Young, M. D. (2016). *A deeper look: INSPIRE data demonstrates quality in educational leadership preparation.* Charlottesville, VA: UCEA.

Weick, K. (1995). *Sensemaking in organizations.* Thousand Oaks, CA: SAGE.

Winerman, L. (2013). Interesting results: Can they be replicated. *Monitor on Psychology, 44*(2), 38.

CHAPTER 5

Bryk, A., Gomez, L., & Grunow, A. (2011). *Getting ideas into action: Building networked improvement communities in education.* Stanford, CA: Carnegie Foundation for the Improvement of Teaching.

Dufour, R., & Eaker, R. (1998). *Professional learning communities at work: Best practices for enhancing student achievement.* Denver, CO: Solution Tree Press.

Hipp, K., & Huffman, J. (2010). Demystifying professional learning communities: School leadership at its best. Lanham, MD: Rowman & Littlefield Education, 11–21.

Hord, S., & Tobia, E. (2012). I am a professional. *The Learning Professional, 33*(3), 16.

Hutchins, E. (1995). *Cognition in the wild.* Cambridge, MA: MIT Press.

Kindt, E., Gijbels, D., Grosemans, I., & Donch, V. (2016). Teachers' everyday professional development: Mapping informal learning activities, antecedents and learning outcomes. *Review of Educational Research, 86*(4), 1111–1150.

Little, J. W. (2002). Locating learning in teachers' communities of practice: Opening up problems of analysis in records of everyday work. *Teaching and Teacher Education, 18,* 917–946.

Louis, K. S., & Kruse, S. D. (1995). *Professionalism and community: Perspectives on reforming urban schools.* Madison: Centre on Organisation and Restructuring of Schools.

Murphy, K., & Knight, S. (2016). Exploring a century of advancement in the science of learning. *Review of Research in Education, 40,* 402–456.

Nehring, J., & Fitzsimons, G. (2011). The professional learning community as subversive activity: Countering the culture of conventional schooling. *Professional Development in Education, 37*(4), 513–535.

Rogoff, B., Callanan, M., Gutierrez, K., & Erickson, F. (2016). The organization of informal learning, *Review of Research in Education*, *40*, 356–401.

Rosenholtz, S. (1985). Effective schools: Interpreting the evidence. *American Journal of Education*, *93*(3), 352–399.

Stoll, L., Bolam, R., Wallace, M, & Thomas, S. (2006). Professional learning communities: A review of the literature, *Journal of Educational Change*, *7*, 221–258.

Wells, C., Fuen, L. (2007). Implementing learning community principles: a study of six high schools, *NASSP Bulletin*, *91*(2), 141–160.

Wenger, E. (1998). *Communities of practice: Learning, meaning, and identity*. Cambridge, England: Cambridge University Press.

CHAPTER 6

Alig-Mielcarek, J. M. (2003). *A model of school success: Instructional leadership, academic press, and student achievement* (Unpublished doctoral dissertation). The Ohio State University, Columbus.

Bandura, A. (1993). Perceived self-efficacy in cognitive development and functioning. *Educational Psychologist*, *28*(2), 117–148.

Benda, S. M. (2000). *The effect of leadership styles on the disciplinary climate and culture of elementary schools* (Unpublished doctoral dissertation). Widener University, Chester, PA.

Brown, B., & Saks, D. (1986). Measuring the effects of instructional time on student learning: Evidence from the Beginning Teacher Evaluation Study. *American Journal of Education*, *94*(4), 480–500.

Bryk, A. & Schneider, B. (2003). Trust in schools: A core resource for school reform. *Educational Leadership*, *60*(6), 40–45.

Carroll, J. (1963). A model of school learning. *Teachers College Record*, *64*(8), 723–733.

Donohoo, J. (2017). *Collective efficacy: How educators' beliefs impact student learning*. Thousand Oaks, CA: Corwin.

Forsyth, P., Adams, C., & Hoy, W. (2011). *Collective trust: Why schools can't improve without it*. New York, NY: Teachers College, Columbia University.

Goddard, R. D. (2003). Relational networks, social trust, and norms: A social capital perspective on students' chances of academic success. *Educational Evaluation and Policy Analysis*, *25*(1), 59–74.

Goddard, R. D., Hoy, W. K., & Hoy, A. W. (2000). Collective teacher efficacy: Its meaning, measure, and impact on student achievement. *American Educational Research Journal*, *37*(2), 479–507.

Goddard, R. D., Tschannen-Moran, M., & Hoy, W. K. (2001). A multilevel examination of the distribution and effects of teacher trust in students and parents in urban elementary schools. *Elementary School Journal*, *102*(1), 3–17.

Goff, P., Goldring, E., Guthrie, J., & Bickman, L. (2014). Changing principals' leadership through feedback and coaching. *Journal of Educational Administration, 52*(5), 682–704.

Gump, S. (2005). The cost of cutting class: Attendance as a predictor of student success. *College Teaching, 53*(1), 21.

Hallinger, P. (1981). *Review of the school effectiveness research*. Prepared for the Carnegie Foundation.

Jacob, J. A. (2004). *A study of school climate and enabling bureaucracy in select New York City public elementary schools* (Unpublished doctoral dissertation). University of Utah, Salt Lake City.

Lavy, V. (2014). Do differences in schools' instructional time explain international achievement gaps? Evidence from developed and developing countries. *Economic Journal, 125*(588), F397–F424.

Lee, V. E., & Smith, J. B. (1999). Social support and achievement for young adolescents in Chicago: The role of school academic press. *American Educational Research Journal, 36*(4), 907–945.

Leithwood, K. (2006). *Working conditions that matter: Evidence for change*. Toronto, Canada: Elementary Teachers Federation of Ontario.

Leithwood, K. (2007). *Taking the project to the next level* (Position paper developed for the LSA Steering Team). Retrieved from https://www.curriculum.org/LSA/files/LSANextLevelAug07.pdf

Leithwood, K., Louis, K., Wahlstrom, K., & Anderson, S. (2004). *Review of research: How leadership influences student learning*. New York, NY: Wallace Foundation.

Ma, X., & Klinger, D. A. (2000). Hierarchical linear modelling of student and school effects on academic achievement. *Canadian Journal of Education, 25*(1), 41–55.

Ma, X., & Willms, J. D. (2004). School disciplinary climate: Characteristics and effects on eighth grade achievement. *Alberta Journal of Educational Research, 50*(2), 169–188.

Malloy, J., & Leithwood, K. (2017). Effects of distributed leadership on school academic press and student achievement, In K. Leithwood, J. Sun, & K. Pollock (Eds.), *How school leaders contribute to student success: The Four Paths Framework*. Dordrecht, The Netherlands: Springer, 69–92.

Marburger, D. (2006). Does mandatory attendance improve student performance? *Journal of Economic Education, 37*(2), 148–155.

Murphy, J. F., Weil, M., Hallinger, P., & Mitman, A. (1982). Academic press: Translating high expectations into school policies and classroom practices. *Educational Leadership, 40*(3), 22–26.

Tschannen-Moran, M., & Barr, M. (2004). Fostering student learning: The relationship of collective teacher efficacy and student achievement. *Leadership and Policy in Schools, 3*(3), 189–209.

Tornroos, J. (2005). Mathematics textbooks, opportunity to learn and student achievement. *Studies in Educational Evaluation, 31*, 315–327.

Wu, J., Hoy, W., & Tarter, J. (2013). Enabling school structure, collective responsibility, and a culture of academic optimism: Toward a robust model of school performance in Taiwan. *Journal of Educational Administration*, *51*(2), 176–193.

CHAPTER 7

Hallinger, P., & Heck, R. (1998). Exploring the principal's contribution to school effectiveness. *School Effectiveness and School Improvement*, *9*(2), 157–165.

Lazowski, R., & Hullemon, C. (2016). Motivation interventions in education. *Review of Educational Research*, *86*(2), 602–640.

Leithwood, K., Anderson, S., Mascall, B., & Strauss, T. (2010). How leaders influence student learning: The four paths. In T. Bush, L. Bell, & D. Middlewood (Eds.), *The principles of educational leadership and management*, 13–30. Thousand Oaks, CA: SAGE.

Leithwood, K., & Louis, K. (2012). *Linking leadership to student learning*. San Francisco, CA: Jossey-Bass.

Leithwood, K., Patten, S., & Jantzi, D. (2010). Testing a conception of how leadership influences student learning. *Educational Administration Quarterly*, *46*(5), 671–706.

Leithwood, K., Sun, J., & Pollock, K. (2017). *How leadership influences student learning: The Four Paths Framework*. New York, NY: Springer Publishers.

Robinson, V., Lloyd, C., & Rowe, K. (2008). The impact of leadership on student outcomes: An analysis of the differential effects of different leadership types. *Educational Administration Quarterly*, *44*(5), 635–674.

CHAPTER 8

Chen, B., & Hong, H.-Y. (2016). Schools as knowledge-building organizations: Thirty years of design research. *Educational Psychologist*, *51*(2), 266–288. doi:10.1080/00461520.2016.1175306

Chen, B., Scardamalia, M., & Bereiter, C. (2015). Advancing knowledge building discourse through judgements of promising ideas. *International Journal of Supported Collaborative Learning*, *10*(4), 345–366.

Dobbie, K., & Frenza, J. (2017). The courage to build knowledge: Taking a leap, In K. Leithwood (Ed.). *Even More Real Stories: How LSA Participation Has Improved Leadership, Teaching and Student Achievement*. Toronto: The Leading Student Achievement Project.

Hattie, J. (2009). *Visible learning: A synthesis of over 800 meta-analyses relating to achievement*. New York, NY: Routledge.

Ma, Y., Matsuzawa, B., Chen, M., & Scardamalia, M. (2016). Transforming learning, empowering learners. *International Conference of the Learning Sciences*, *1*, 615–622.

Resendes, M., & Dobbie, K. (2017a). *Knowledge building gallery: Teaching for deep understanding and community knowledge creation* (A collection of foundational KB practices and teacher innovations). Toronto, Canada: Leading Student Achievement: Networks for Learning Project.

Resendes, M., & Dobbie, K. (2017b). *Knowledge building in action.* Toronto, Canada: Leading Student Achievement: Networks for Learning Project.

Resendes, M., Scardamalia, M., Bereiter, C., Chen, B., & Halewood, C. (2015). Group-level formative feedback and metadiscourse. *International Journal of Supported Collaborative Learning, 10*(3), 309–336.

Scardamalia, M. (2002). Collective cognitive responsibility for the advancement of knowledge. In B. Smith & C. Bereiter (Eds.), *Liberal education in a knowledge society* (pp. 67–98). Berkeley, CA: Publishers Group West.

Scardamalia, M., & Bereiter, C. (2006). Knowledge building and knowledge creation: Theory, pedagogy, and technology. In K. Sawyer (Ed.), *Cambridge handbook of the learning sciences* (pp. 97–118). Cambridge, England: Cambridge University Press.

Scardamalia, M., Bereiter, C., Brett, C., Burtis, P. J., Calhoun, C., & Smith Lea, N. (1992). Educational applications of a networked communal database. *Interactive Learning Environments, 2*(1), 45–71.

Wahlstrom, K., & Louis, K. (2008). How teachers experience principal leadership: The role of professional community, trust, efficacy and shared responsibility. *Educational Administration Quarterly, 44*(4), 458–495.

Waler, C., Fehrman, S., Hahn, W., Kosh. K., Milani, M., Oakes, L., Sendzik, M., Webb, S., & Zwolak, M., Our principal journey. In K. Leithwood (Ed.). *More Real Stories: How LSA Participation Has Improved Leadership, Teaching and Student Achievement.* Toronto: The Leading Student Achievement Project.

CHAPTER 9

Leithwood, K., & Azah, V. (2016). Characteristics of effective leadership networks. *Journal of Educational Administration, 55*, 1.

CHAPTER 10

Berman, P., & McLaughlin, M. (1978). *Federal Programs Supporting Educational Change. Vol. VIII: Implementing and sustaining innovations.* Santa Monica, CA: RAND.

Brown, A., Stacey, P., & Nandhakumar, J. (2007). Making sense of sense making narratives. *Human Relations, 61*(8), 1035–1062.

Bryk, A. S., Bender Sebring, P., Allensworth, E., Luppescu, S., & Easton, J. Q. (2010). *Organizing schools for improvement: Lessons from Chicago*. Chicago, IL: University of Chicago.

Gates, S., Hamilton, L., Mortorell, P., Burkhauser, S., Pierson, A., Baird, M., . . . Kun Gu, M. (2014). *Preparing principals to raise student achievement: Implementation and effects of the New Leaders Program in ten districts*. Santa Monica, CA: RAND Corporation.

Goddard, R. D., Sweetland, S. R., & Hoy, W. K. (2000). Academic emphasis of urban elementary schools and student achievement in reading and mathematics: A multilevel analysis. *Educational Administration Quarterly, 36*(5), 683–702.

Hargreaves, A., & Fullan, M. (2012). *Professional capital: Transforming teaching in every school*. New York, NY: Teachers College Press.

Jacob, R., Goddard, R. D., Kim, M., Miller, R. J., & Goddard, Y. L. (2015). Exploring the causal impact of the McREL Balanced Leadership Program on leadership, principal efficacy, instructional climate, educator turnover, and student achievement. *Educational Evaluation and Policy Analysis, 37*, 314–332.

Leithwood, K. (2012). *The Ontario Leadership Framework: With a discussion of the research foundations*. Toronto, Canada: Institute for Educational Leadership.

Leithwood, K., Riedlinger, B., & Bauer, S. (2003). Leadership program effects on student learning: The case of the Greater New Orleans School Leadership Centre. *Journal of School Leadership, 13*(6), 707–738.

Lieberman, A., & Grolnick, M. (1996). Networks and reform in American education. *Teachers College Record, 98*(1), 7–45.

Louis, K. S., & Lee, M. (2016). Teachers' capacity for organizational learning: The effects of school culture and context. *School Effectiveness and School Improvement, 27*(4), 534–556.

Nunnery, J. A., Ross, S. M., & Yen, C. (2010a). *An examination of the effect of a pilot of the National Institute for School Leadership's Executive Development Program on school performance trends in Massachusetts*. Norfolk, VA: Center for Educational Partnerships.

Nunnery, J., Ross, S.M., & Yen, C. (2010b). *The effect of the National Institute for School Leadership's Executive Development Program on school performance trends in Pennsylvania*. Norfolk, VA: Center for Educational Partnerships at Old Dominion University.

Robinson, V., Lloyd, C., & Rowe, K. (2008). The impact of leadership on student outcomes: An analysis of the differential effects of leadership types. *Educational Administration Quarterly, 44*(5), 564–588.

INDEX

CORWIN
LEADERSHIP

Anthony Kim & Alexis Gonzales-Black
Designed to foster flexibility and continuous innovation, this resource expands cutting-edge management and organizational techniques to empower schools with the agility and responsiveness vital to their new environment.

Jonathan Eckert
Explore the collective and reflective approach to progress, process, and programs that will build conditions that lead to strong leadership and teaching, which will improve student outcomes.

PJ Caposey
Offering a fresh perspective on teacher evaluation, this book guides administrators to transform their school culture and evaluation process to improve teacher practice and, ultimately, student achievement.

Dwight L. Carter & Mark White
Through understanding the past and envisioning the future, the authors use practical exercises and real-life examples to draw the blueprint for adapting schools to the age of hyper-change.

Raymond L. Smith & Julie R. Smith
This solid, sustainable, and laser-sharp focus on instructional leadership strategies for coaching might just be your most impactful investment toward student achievement.

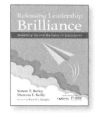

Simon T. Bailey & Marceta F. Reilly
This engaging resource provides a simple, sustainable framework that will help you move your school from mediocrity to brilliance.

Debbie Silver & Dedra Stafford
Equip educators to develop resilient and mindful learners primed for academic growth and personal success.

Peter Gamwell & Jane Daly
Discover a new perspective on how to nurture creativity, innovation, leadership, and engagement.

Leadership That Makes an Impact

Steven Katz, Lisa Ain Dack, & John Malloy
Leverage the oppositional forces of top-down expectations and bottom-up experience to create an intelligent, responsive school.

Peter M. DeWitt
Centered on staff efficacy, these resources present discussion questions, vignettes, strategies, and action steps to improve school climate, leadership collaboration, and student growth.

Eric Sheninger
Harness digital resources to create a new school culture, increase communication and student engagement, facilitate real-time professional growth, and access new opportunities for your school.

Russell J. Quaglia, Kristine Fox, Deborah Young, Michael J. Corso, & Lisa L. Lande
Listen to your school's voice to see how you can increase engagement, involvement, and academic motivation.

Michael Fullan, Joanne Quinn, & Joanne McEachen
Learn the right drivers to mobilize complex, coherent, whole-system change and transform learning for all students.

CORWIN LEADERSHIP

A SAGE Publishing Company

Helping educators make the greatest impact

CORWIN HAS ONE MISSION: to enhance education through intentional professional learning.

We build long-term relationships with our authors, educators, clients, and associations who partner with us to develop and continuously improve the best evidence-based practices that establish and support lifelong learning.

Leading Student Achievement: Networks for Learning gratefully acknowledges the leadership of the three principals' associations - l'Association des directions et directions adjointes des écoles franco-ontariennes), Catholic Principals' Council | Ontario and Ontario Principals' Council, in partnership and funded by the Student Achievement Division, Ontario Ministry of Education.

Association des directions et directions adjointes des écoles franco-ontariennes

L'Association des directions et directions adjointes des écoles franco-ontariennes est l'association professionnelle pour environ 600 directions et directions adjointes œuvrant dans les écoles de langue française de l'Ontario, tant publiques que catholiques. L'ADFO appuie l'apprentissage professionnel des directions, notamment en matière de leadership, afin que tous nos leaders continuent de contribuer à l'amélioration du rendement et du bien-être de chacun des élèves.

Catholic Principals' Council Ontario is a professional, non-profit association serving over 2,100 Principals and Vice-Principals in Ontario's 29 publicly-funded Catholic school boards. CPCO, called to leadership in Catholic education through service and advocacy with a commitment to gospel values, is a leading Catholic educational association in Canada, providing high-quality professional learning and leadership development for Catholic school leaders.

The Ontario Principals' Council (OPC) is a voluntary professional association representing 5,000 practising school leaders in elementary and secondary schools across Ontario. We believe that exemplary leadership results in outstanding schools and improved student achievement. We foster quality leadership through world-class professional services and supports, striving to continuously achieve "quality leadership - our principal product."